T0279453

Praise for *CARE to Win*

"Quiet quitting, hybrid workplace, toxic boss . . . How do you lead today? A good place to start is by reading this book. This fresh look at leadership cannot be ignored, shouldn't be denied, and must be taken to heart. *CARE to Win* will show you the importance of caring as a leader of today."

—Keith Ferrazzi, Founder, Chairman, and CEO
of Ferrazzi Greenlight and *New York Times* Bestselling
Author of *Who's Got Your Back?* and *Never Eat Alone*

"My favorite part of this excellent new leadership book is the beginning of the chapter on Autonomy: '"I love being told how to do my job!" said no one ever. Equally popular is the experience of being micromanaged. Overmanagement puts shackles on your creativity and capability. To be given Autonomy is to be given freedom. And trust.' The value of trusting your team cannot be overstated."

—Dave Kerpen, *New York Times* Bestselling
Author of *Get Over Yourself*

"The CARE Equation is exactly what high-performing leaders need to build high-performing teams. Make the commitment to practice CARE daily, and you'll be rewarded with higher engagement and retention."

—Shep Hyken, *New York Times* Bestselling
Author of *The Amazement Revolution*

"Alex Draper's CARE Equation is a simple, but powerful, formula. There's a wealth of research behind how Clarity, Autonomy, Relationships, and Equity create motivation and enhance performance. This book is refreshingly practical in each approach to living out each element."

—Dr. David Burkus, Bestselling and Award-Winning
Author of *Best Team Ever* and *Leading from Anywhere*

"As a branding strategist and executive coach, I have experienced firsthand the critical importance of psychological safety in building winning brands and successful company cultures. As Alex says, 'Psychological safety is the key ingredient to unleashing human potential.' The book shows leaders practical ways they can achieve this state for their staff and companies. I would recommend it for new managers and experienced C-suite alike."

—Karen Tiber Leland, Bestselling Author of *The Brand Mapping Strategy: Design, Build, and Accelerate Your Brand*

"I love this book and the messages it offers. The CARE Equation is simple: Clarity, Autonomy, Relationships, and Equity. And the descriptions of each, along with the biases they create, are straightforward. It would benefit *all* leaders to CARE a little more in the workplace, and this book will help you get started."

—Lisa Bodell, CEO of FutureThink and Award-Winning Author of *Kill the Company* and *Why Simple Wins*

"Alex Draper has done far more than write a book on the mechanics of building leadership for high-performance teamwork; he has provided a working template on HOW to develop both yourself as a leader and also your team. Having worked as a consultant and coach for more than forty years and as the author of four books, I can tell you that his CARE Equation, as he unpacks it, is both brilliant and highly practical. He has captured, in a concise and highly organized manner, what takes most people (if they are very attentive and diligent) decades of practice to learn. Here is a book on the WHAT, the HOW, and the WHO of creating sustainable high-performance teams."

—Robert E. Staub II, Founder and CEO of EQIQ Leadership and Author of *The Heart of Leadership* and *The 7 Acts of Courage*

"It's not possible to remind leaders too much about the foundational leadership principle of taking care of their people. Taking the best of the latest research in positive leadership and management, Founder of DX Learning, Alex Draper's book demonstrates what is possible in teams and organizations by taking a people-centered approach. Draper's CARE Equation is what leaders need to succeed in a rapidly changing world. An important book for leaders in any industry committed to making a difference in the world through their leadership."

—Shannon Huffman Polson, Founder and CEO of the Grit Institute and Author of *The Grit Factor: Courage, Resilience, and Leadership in the Most Male-Dominated Organization in the World*

"As the CEO of my own company and close advisor to many other CEOs, I've spent much of the last several years understanding how to create, propagate, and reinforce psychological safety—it is the *single* most important factor in a positive company culture. All great teams are centered in psychological safety, which requires strong, active communication. Alex provides an excellent framework for companies to adapt to strengthen their teams and performance. It can be a strategic advantage for any team that deploys it. This book should be part of any new manager's training and on the desk of every leader, from the C-suite to the front line."

—Lee Caraher, CEO of Double Forte, Speaker, and Author of *Millennials and Management* and *The Boomerang Principle*

"As an executive coach who lives by relationships, I was anxious to see what Draper had to say about them. I couldn't have agreed more when I read, 'For the sake of this playbook, let's define relationships as demonstrating you care by connecting with your team on a human level.' He expounded on it with, 'That means changing your focus from results-first to people-first. When you put people first and results second, you end up fostering a team that creates the best results anyway—far better than when you put results first.' While this is a great book throughout, this seemed particularly insightful."

—Dr. Mark Goulston, Marshall Goldsmith 100 Coach and Author of *Just Listen*

"Drawing on foundational insights, sharing relevant stories, and offering actionable tools, Alex advances leadership effectiveness by ensuring psychological safety through Clarity, Autonomy, Relationships, and Equity. He demonstrates using this formula in his work and how it can be applied for any leader seeking to improve."

—**Dave Ulrich, Author of *HR from the Outside In*; Co-Founder and Partner of the RBL Group; and Professor and Director at Stephen M. Ross School of Business, University of Michigan**

"Too often, approaches to develop leadership fail as they don't enable leaders to truly understand themselves or others better. From my neuroscience studies, I know it's absolutely vital that to be effective and optimize the power of people, leaders need to understand what's going on psychologically as well as practically. Alex combines both in a way that brings clarity so that anyone can read, reflect, and take action to be more successful."

—**Chris Roebuck, Global Leadership Expert and Speaker, Ten-Time Award Winner of "HR Most Influential Thinker" Title, and Hon Visiting Professor of Transformational Leadership**

"At the heart of Draper's book is a simple truth: people matter most. The CARE framework is a tangible roadmap for people-centric leadership that nurtures the human element in every interaction. It's not only aligned our own leadership team, but also reinvigorated our organization with a growth mindset, sense of purpose, and empathy. This is a go-to read for leaders who aim to release the untapped potential of their teams and shape the future of corporate culture."

—**Cindy Donohoe, EVP and Chief Marketing Officer, Highmark Health**

"I absolutely love this book! A powerful and thought-provoking read that has the potential to transform the way we lead and create high-performing organizations. It offers practical guidance on achieving

Clarity, embracing Autonomy, nurturing Relationships, and striving for Equity—all key ingredients to becoming a highly effective leader. I highly recommend it to anyone seeking personal and professional growth. Enjoy it!"

—Ricardo Leite, Senior Vice President and Head of
International Markets at Discover Financial Services

"I love the CARE framework. It creates a simple but very powerful shared language to engage teams and organizations. We found the CARE Equation to be impactful for all people: from leaders in the C-suite to our frontline leaders. If you lead teams, you should read this book. Every leader has a responsibility to CARE so their teams CARE back."

—Jeff Krautkramer, Chief Human Resource Officer of Madison Air

"This framework Alex offers—which is simple, clear, and memorable— makes it that much easier to change the way you approach leadership. This change is important because leadership is *not* about you, it's about everyone else! The Alexamples sprinkled throughout the book are real and meaningful changes you can make to bring real impact in your organization. I have used this framework with real teams in the real world and can wholeheartedly say it works!"

—Jane Urban, Vice President, Customer Engagement Operations,
Otsuka Americas Pharmaceuticals Inc.

"This book will reconfigure your thoughts on leadership. How leaders are made versus born, what leaders do in the complex workplace, and how they create clarity for their teams. Many of the paradigms we have about leaders and leadership are dated and unsustainable. My favorite part of the book sums up leadership best to me: 'Would all your people see you as a leader that deliberately and intentionally sends everyone home less stressed and feeling like they left nothing on the table?'"

—Derick Faulkner, Director of HR at Eaton Corporation

"Creating psychological safety in the workplace is critical to people achieving their best—professionally and personally. In Draper's book, he cogently describes how to overcome bias to become a leader that others will flock to, while also helping your team achieve its greatest performance."

—Jenna Fisher, Managing Director of Russell Reynolds Associates

"*CARE to Win: The Four Leadership Habits to Build High-Performing Teams* is a must-read for leaders and managers seeking to foster a positive and thriving work environment. Alex Draper's CARE Equation provides a practical and research-backed playbook that will empower you to create a culture of psychological safety where employees feel valued, heard, and motivated to achieve their highest potential."

—Jeff DeGraff, PhD, Clinical Professor, Stephen M. Ross School of Business, University of Michigan

CARE to Win

CARE
to Win

The **4** Leadership Habits to
Build High-Performing Teams

Alex Draper

BROWN BOOKS
PUBLISHING GROUP

CARE to Win
The 4 Leadership Habits to Build High-Performing Teams

Brown Books Publishing Group
Dallas, TX / New York, NY
www.BrownBooks.com
(972) 381-0009

A New Era in Publishing®

Publisher's Cataloging-In-Publication Data

Names: Draper, Alex, author.
Title: CARE to win : the 4 leadership habits to build high-performing teams /
    Alex Draper.
Description: Dallas, TX ; New York, NY : Brown Books Publishing Group, [2024]
    | Includes bibliographical references.
Identifiers: ISBN: 978-1-61254-674-2 | LCCN: 2023950068
Subjects: LCSH: Leadership. | Work environment--Psychological aspects. |
    Teams in the workplace. | Psychology, Industrial. | Industrial productivity.
    | Employee loyalty. | Success in business. | BISAC: BUSINESS &
    ECONOMICS / Leadership. | SELF-HELP / Personal Growth / Success.
Classification: LCC: HD57.7 .D73 2024 | DDC: 658.4092--dc23

ISBN 978-1-61254-674-2
LCCN 2023950068

Printed in Canada
10 9 8 7 6 5 4 3 2 1

For more information or to contact the author, please go to www.Alex-Draper.com.

To my young and still innocent kids, Dominic and Victoria, I wrote this book to try to make sure you enter a workplace where you will be treated properly—reflective of the people you both are. We get such a short time on this planet. Being mistreated by your boss or anyone else for that matter should not be something you should have to worry about. It is my hope that you don't ever have to go through some of the things I have had to witness and sometimes endure. To me, it would be a significant accomplishment for your boss to read this book and make the decision to CARE for you as I have tried to. What I hope and would love for both of you is to be CARE champions to all those you serve, as I have worked hard to be. Even if I didn't win at this every time, I certainly did my very best to. Carry the CARE flag and make the world a little less stressful to live and work.

CONTENTS

PART III: RELATIONSHIPS

PART IV: EQUITY

FOREWORD

By Dr. Marshall Goldsmith

My mission for over forty years as an executive coach is to help successful leaders get even better for their teams, companies, and lives. My motivation has never been for fame or accolades but rather a profound desire to help others. As I dove into *CARE to Win: The Four Leadership Habits to Build High-Performing Teams*, it was immediately apparent that Alex is a kindred spirit, motivated by the pure intent of helping people.

This book isn't your typical, dry leadership manual; it reads more like a coaching session. Alex encourages you to embrace a growth mindset, confront your blind spots, and continuously strive for betterment. It's a style that closely aligns with my own coaching philosophy.

One of the book's standout qualities is Alex's candid sharing of his own missteps and vulnerabilities. It's an acknowledgment that, in the end, we're all human, bound to stumble along the way. What truly matters is the wisdom we gain from these experiences. As someone who has walked a similar path, I find Alex's stories and lessons deeply relatable.

As the founder of DX Learning, Alex introduces us to the profound philosophy he's developed as a leader in real situations: the CARE Equation. This is a four-part playbook that revolves around the role of psychological safety in high-performing teams. The book eloquently illustrates that leaders bear the responsibility for nurturing this environment, where employees can comfortably express themselves, ultimately flourishing in their roles.

In the realm of management theories, we've progressed far beyond outdated paradigms like Theory X. Alex introduces an elegant concept: caring for your people. It's a straightforward yet profound idea that encapsulates effective leadership, a concept you'll find masterfully explored in this book.

The four elements of CARE—Clarity, Autonomy, Relationships, and Equity—form the bedrock for high-performing teams. They ensure alignment, empowerment, appreciation, and fairness, countering the chaos of miscommunication or the stifling grip of micromanagement. Notably, the Relationships element underscores the importance of valuing team members as unique individuals, recognizing their diverse backgrounds and experiences. It's a fundamental human need to be appreciated, not reduced to mere resources, and Alex brilliantly highlights this point.

Equity, the final element, is where many leaders stumble. Alex expertly distinguishes Equity from Equality, emphasizing the importance of tailoring resources to individual needs—an idea particularly relevant in today's discussions on fairness and inclusion.

A crucial topic of Alex's book, and one that particularly needs to be addressed in today's business environment, is his exploration of biases that can hinder our embrace of CARE. For each element of CARE, he identifies two biases, explains their effects, and provides remedies. These practical insights, complemented by real-world examples and detailed guidance on overcoming biases, are invaluable additions to any leader's toolkit.

As someone who has spent years coaching and educating executives, I can attest to the transformative potential of understanding how beliefs and environments influence behaviors. *CARE to Win* is a powerful resource that I wholeheartedly recommend to executives and leaders at all levels. Its profound wisdom and focus on the science of leadership will undoubtedly guide you in becoming a better leader while fostering a more compassionate and successful world.

I invite you to embark on this enlightening journey through Alex Draper's world of CARE. It's not just a path to high-performance teams; it's a roadmap to creating a culture marked by empathy, support, and kindness. Enjoy your reading and remember that every page brings you a step closer to CARE.

Dr. Marshall Goldsmith
Top Thinkers50-Ranked Executive Coach and
New York Times Bestselling Author of *The Earned Life*,
Triggers, and *What Got You Here Won't Get You There*

INTRODUCTION

Another book on leadership? Yes, but before you banish this one to the Great Shelf of Unread Leadership Books (you know, the one that proudly sits behind you on every Zoom call), let me make you a promise: if you put the ideas in this book into practice, you *will* have a higher-performing team.

High-performing teams need high-performing leaders in order to win. Win at what? Well, that depends on what you want. It could be the knowledge that you have become a better leader. That your team is more engaged. Your sales numbers have improved. Your retention of great team members improves. You get that promotion you dreamed of.

What do you want to win at?

To win, you need to CARE. No, not the cuddly type. The CARE I'm talking about are the human skills that get the hard stuff done. As you will find out, when you CARE, you and your team will perform better, and those goals that you have, you'll be able to achieve them. You can win by implementing the CARE Equation intentionally, daily, and consistently over the next year. In that time, you will become the high-performing leader your team needs. Your engagement scores and retention rates will rise substantially—perhaps even shockingly. Your relationships, both at work and at home, will improve. And those who work around you will consider you a vastly improved human being. They might even call you their best boss ever.

Growing up in the UK, I moved to America for work in 2002, and since then I've travelled the world delivering thousands of leadership-development programs and coaching hundreds of leaders. I have witnessed firsthand some great leaders, though many more not-so-great ones have been the norm. I started my company, DX Learning, because I was tired of dealing with "leaders" who talked a good leadership game on LinkedIn and coaching calls, at the training events I run, and even in meetings and conferences, but still continued to act like—I'll use the indelicate word—*a**holes* on a day-to-day basis. I've been on the receiving end of a**hole leadership in my jobs, and I myself was in danger of becoming one of those leaders—until I found an astonishingly simple yet effective way to evaluate myself and how I was leading. By implementing these steps, I was able to actually *care* about the people I work with (and my family at home) while improving business results. People stopped dreading interactions with me and began to stick around long enough to get things done and achieve new goals. When I started to care, so did they, and this equation became part of our daily routine that drastically changed me and DX for the better.

That effective four-step way is called, appropriately enough, the CARE Equation.

My Team's Journey to Psychological Safety and Higher Performance

One of the most humbling experiences of my career came when the world first went into the COVID-19 quarantine lockdown in March of 2020. Almost overnight, I was in jeopardy of losing everything.

Our business model was that of an in-person leadership development firm. My strong belief (bias, assumption . . .) was that effective leadership development needed to be delivered as an in-person event. Which, of course, meant that when people suddenly weren't allowed to leave their houses except for basic survival needs, we lost a lot of business. I mean a *lot*! We ended up with zero revenue for four months. All my new gray hair stands as a testament.

There were days when I literally had no idea how I was going to fund payroll, unsure whether my credit cards had enough wiggle room to afford fuel and food for me and my family. Of course, my survival brain was telling me to take care of myself, shut the doors, fire everyone, and save the cash for myself. But I didn't. My company adapted, and we survived. I learned a great deal about my own weaknesses and how hard it is to be a great leader, but it's in those moments when the s**t hits the fan that you really find out what leaders are made of and what type of leader you really are.

Our organization's dedication to creating a psychologically safe culture is the reason we survived the COVID-19 pandemic. We were able to tear down our old business model, innovate, and work together to build a new model. Because of the psychological safety we've established, we spoke up and shared ideas about what was working and what was not. We felt comfortable enough to fail quickly and learn.

I developed this playbook back in 2018, well before the pandemic, and it took eighteen months of leading in an inclusive and empathetic (i.e., CAREing) way to get my team at DX Learning to be in a place where they openly spoke up and were able to give me, and each other, the candid feedback we needed to grow and develop. This is what saved us from going under in 2020. Not CAREing could have cost my people their jobs and me my company and livelihood. I would like to say we are now a team that is *always* willing to be vulnerable, openly share our mistakes and failures, and talk about what is working and what is not—but we're not quite there yet. We're getting closer every day, and I think that's the best you can ever do.

But how do I know we are still a high-performing team? In 2022—only two years after nearly losing it all—we made it into *Training Industry*'s list of top forty leadership training companies. Not bad for a company that was in business less than seven years. I attribute that primarily to building a psychologically safe place for the team to do their best work and be their best selves. I couldn't reach this height alone; no leader can. I am not a hero, and a "solo hero" mentality doesn't ever work in business. It's through the power of psychological safety that we all succeed together and how we got to where we are now.

There's a mutual expectation on my team that we speak up early and often—we all have a voice, and silence is not something often heard on our team calls. Trust me, it takes concerted effort to create this level of safety that a team is willing to be open, honest, and receptive. It doesn't just happen with a snap of the fingers. Creating a high-performing culture centered around the idea of psychological safety requires two things: first, a deliberate, leader-charged strategy; second, the whole team must buy into the idea for it to work.

What to Expect

My goal in writing this book is to unleash the leadership potential you have within you, whether you lead a corporation, a small or large team, a client, or supplier—even a family, a book or soccer club, or a partnership of two people. I want you to be a leader who treats other people as the humans they are while enabling the whole team to thrive. I want you to become aware of some of the biases you carry in your brain, which can keep you stuck in selfish-leader mode, and to ultimately help *you* be the best leader and person *you* can be. Your self-centered, keep-me-safe, help-me-win brain plays tricks on you every day, trying to ensure you do what is best for *you*. But leadership is not about you. It's about others.

Read that again: Leadership is not about you. It's about others.

The great thing is that when you consistently and intentionally follow the CARE Equation and CARE for others, others CARE for you. It's a shift of mindset that requires you to wake up and combat the selfish and CAREless brain. Throughout this book, we will look at some intriguing scientific findings about how the brain works. As we cover the four components of CARE—Clarity, Autonomy, Relationships, and Equity®—we will explore two common cognitive biases that often get in the way of achieving each part. We'll also talk about how to overcome these biases so you can put *your* best foot forward. Recognizing and challenging your biases will be the key to becoming the most CAREing leader possible.

I wrote this book to help others learn from my mistakes. I've made a ton of them. The mistakes I made early on resulted in the loss of many team members. In fact, no one who was part of my company in the beginning (except me) is still around today. However, I turned the ship around by not *talking* about the fact that I CARE but by actually CAREing every day. This entailed—and still does—doing the hard work of challenging my biases. Throughout this book, I'll share some of these moments called "Alexamples" where I, had I been the CAREing leader I strive to be, could've saved me a lot of headaches and stress and will use them to show CARE in action—how it leads to a psychologically safe environment for high-performing teams.

The culture of your team, more than ever, is a mirror of *you*.

How you think, speak, and behave will dictate how others think, speak, and behave. If you are confident, your team will be confident. If you are stressed, your team will be stressed. If you don't lead effectively, your team won't run effectively. The worst behaviors you are willing to tolerate become engrained in the culture. Leadership is how *you* choose to positively influence others and hold them accountable to the standards you believe are right. CARE is how you do it effectively. You have a huge amount of influence on others. Use it wisely, and leave a humbling shadow in your path.

So, let's dig in.

Accomplishing such effective leadership means you must embrace CARE as a set of daily habits. To help you along the journey, I have created an exclusive members area for book purchasers that will give you access to habit-forming technology, exclusive videos, on-the-job tools, and ways to communicate your learnings to those you serve. Scan the QR code and enter your email to access free content that supports the lessons you are about to read about.

CHAPTER 1

BIASES—THE ULTIMATE THREAT TO
HIGHER PERFORMANCE

A leader must serve others and care for the people they serve. The more they do that, the more their team will care back. The more the team cares back, the higher performing everyone will be. That is the essence of *CARE to Win.*

It sounds simple. And it is. But there's one major hurdle to overcome: your brain. True leaders must serve others, but the human brain, unfortunately, is designed to serve itself. And it's jam-packed with biases to help it do so. This often makes even the best of intending leaders to come off as unintentional a**holes—especially when they feel like they're doing the best job they can. Fortunately, your brain can be retrained with a bit of effort by reading this book and listening to my mistakes. But how do you know if you're the a**hole when your brain is telling you you're doing a great job?

AITA (Am I the A**hole)?
For the sake of this book, let's define a**hole as someone who comes across as caught up in their own stuff. That might not be their true and full nature, but that is how they are perceived by others. They don't know that they are viewed that way, so they don't have a plan to change this. And if they're not a growth-minded leader, they probably won't be picking up this book to learn their biases and how

best to combat them. So they are continuously seen by their peers as putting their own needs first and treating others mainly as a means to achieving their own ends. They don't seem to see other people for who they really are or hear what they have to say. It's the mentality of "me" instead of "we."

In most cases, it's not because a**holes are terrible people; it's because they are following the mandates of their selfishly designed brains, which is the most natural thing in the world to do, it turns out, and no one dares to tell them otherwise. Some might truthfully say being an a**hole comes naturally. That wouldn't be a problem if it weren't for the fact that *other people* stubbornly insist upon existing in this world. Other people whose help and talents we need. Other people who have their own goals and values and agendas. Other people who do not respond well to narcissistic leadership.

A Selfish Brain Is a Bias-Driven Brain

For most of the three hundred thousand years we have walked this planet, we have been hunter-gatherers. Because we've had to fight for our food, water, shelter—basic survival really—our brains are wired to keep us alive. To function effectively, we've created thousands of mental shortcuts called *heuristics* to solve problems, make decisions, and make judgments quickly and effectively to keep us alive. This way, we process information quickly without stopping and thinking what long-term effects it might have, but it ensures we have enough mental resources to survive in the moment, as the brain's primary function is to scan for threats. After all, it is more important to know where the nearest predator is than the nearest blueberry. (And those early humans who couldn't make this distinction didn't stick around long enough to evolve into late humans.)

Threat Detection

For present-day humans that are running advanced society software (modern technology) and taking care of their teams using only their caveman hardware (our brain), these heuristics still get in the way. Our brain's "processor" isn't hardwired well enough for the twenty-first-century workplace because heuristics try to do things as easily and automatically as possible. Taking the path of least resistance. In short, being lazy. A lazy leader won't help your team win.

There *is* a good reason for the brain's heuristics. If we were to consciously process all the stimuli our brains take in every second, our heads would explode. Not literally, of course—but that's what it would feel like. We would have no processing power left for our creative or productive tasks. Heuristics are vital to our survival and success, but they are also broad and lack nuance.

To illustrate this point, let's try a quick exercise inspired by Daniel Kahneman, the psychologist and author of *Thinking, Fast and Slow*. Imagine that a notepad and pencil together cost $1.10. The notepad costs one dollar more than the pencil. How much does each item cost?

Your speedy answer was likely that the pencil costs ten cents, and the notepad costs a dollar. That seems logical based on the brain's shortcut thinking. But upon more careful reflection, you realize the cost of the pencil is actually five cents. The notepad, $1.05.

Heuristics can easily lead us to assumptions that are not always accurate. These negative results of our heuristics are often known as *biases*.

Brain researchers have documented over 188 cognitive biases in the human brain to date, though we'll never know the exact number, of course. Most of these brain shortcuts were designed for our survival—scan for threats, keep us safe—so we could use our processing power for other things. Now those threats have changed from saber-toothed tigers to bosses with oversized egos, but your brain is still designed to focus on your own well-being. It processes anywhere from eleven million to twenty *trillion* bits of information per second.[1]

Seriously.

Per. Second.

To do that, the brain really does need to make a *lot* of assumptions. And when we don't take control of those assumptions, it can lead to some unfortunate outcomes between people. That's because the brain is designed to keep *you* safe—not anyone else. But what is leadership all about? The exact *opposite*. Leadership is about keeping *others* safe. Doing what's best for others. Putting others first—not you.

Hmm . . .

> ## Leadership is about keeping others safe.

Naturally, your brain doesn't like that. And that's why it's accurate to say no one is born to be a leader. To be a great leader, you must literally do the opposite of what your brain is telling you to do much of the time. The main challenge for leaders is that it's always quicker and easier to assume something than it is to stop, think, and really try to "know" something. Your brain wants to move on to the next task, not spend your energy, which is vital for survival, on people that are not you. This is good for you and you alone—not the people you work with. You must fight those 188+ biases to become the leader that helps their team win. Here is a list of twenty that you may be familiar with:

1. Negativity Bias
2. Confirmation Bias
3. Recency Illusion
4. Placebo Effect
5. Stereotyping
6. Authority Bias
7. Halo Effect
8. Positivity Bias
9. Not Invented Here
10. Murphy's Law
11. Zero-Sum Bias
12. Illusion of Transparency
13. Projection Bias
14. Proximity Bias
15. Overconfidence Effect
16. Sunk-Cost Fallacy
17. Loss Aversion
18. Status Quo Bias
19. Primacy Effect
20. Google Effect

Anyone who says they are "not biased" simply doesn't know how the brain works. You don't get rid of biases. We are all susceptible to them, and while we think we are less biased than the next person (one universal bias), in reality, we are *all* assumption-making machines. These 188—or more—biases are flaws that keep us from making the right choices quite often. This isn't because we have bad intentions; it's because we have no idea how to do things differently. We have blind spots. And unless someone shows us a different way—unless we gain greater self-awareness—we just keep on doing the best we can from our limited perspective and caveman hardware.

Human instinct is self-preservation. Leadership is team preservation. As the illustration below shows, your brain is selfish. Its own safety, not the safety of others, comes first. You need to fight that instinctive wiring so you can be a selfless, team-orientated leader.

> Human instinct is self-preservation. Leadership is team preservation.

What Is Leadership?

Before we go any further, let's get aligned on what "leadership" is and what it isn't.

Common misconceptions: Leadership is just for C-suite executives. Leadership and management are two different things. Leaders are a "special breed."

My definition of leadership: One human being positively influencing another.

The truth is, we are all leaders. Leadership is not a specialized category of human endeavor. We all need to influence others, whether in big or small ways. Opportunities for leadership abound in every facet of our lives. Even if you don't have anyone directly reporting to you, you are still a leader. If you are a salesperson trying to close a sale, you are a leader. If you are a physician trying to influence a patient, you are a leader. A CEO is a leader and so is a shop-floor supervisor. Teachers, parents, consultants, directors, managers—all are leaders. Leadership is an integral part of life.

Leadership is for everyone, not just those with leadership titles, and it can be implemented in everything you do. Leadership is simply a choice you make to wake up in the morning and say, "Today I am going to positively influence others."

It's the word "positively" that I want you to focus on in your own leadership. Most of us have a tendency to fall back on negative forms of influence, especially when we need a job done *now*. We criticize, we blame, we rage, we manipulate, we employ fear, we express disappointment. Those techniques may work, to some extent, in the very short run, but they have a tremendous cost in the long run. Think of your top performing team member(s). Would you miss them if they left tomorrow? Or do they become actively disengaged and gossip behind your back, bringing the performance of the whole team down? Either way, it will cost you more time, money, or performance. That is when you know you have lost—when your best people leave (mentally or physically) due to you unintentionally mistreating them. In this book, I'll delve deeply into the positive practices you can do as a culture champion and thought leader, and it's all about CAREing for others.

Positive Leadership = Effective Leadership

Think about your favorite boss of all time. What was it about them that made them your favorite? Make a quick list of their traits.

I'll bet your list didn't include that they worked hard. They were supremely intelligent and talked a lot. Or that they were amazing at spreadsheets!

I'll bet most of the things on your list had to do with human skills. *They had my back. They developed and coached me. They were honest. They were inclusive. They made me feel good about myself. They gave me confidence.*

One of my favorite quotes from Maya Angelou:

> "I've learned that people will forget what you said, people will forget what you did, but people will never forget how you made them feel."[2]

That's what great leadership is about: how you make people feel at the end of the day.

Do you want to be on your team's list of favorite bosses of all time? To achieve that, you need to be an effective leader, and effective leaders these days absolutely must have excellent human skills. The human skills are the ones that get

> **The human skills are the ones that get the hard stuff done.**

the hard stuff done. Human skills are the essentials needed to connect and communicate effectively with other people—things like feedback, trust, empathy, inclusion, adaptability, and clear communication. Used well, these skills provide more to those you serve than yourself because human skills are selfless skills that make others feel good about themselves. In order to build these human (selfless) skills, you need to CARE. (We'll define this acronym in a minute.) But again, the problem is our selfish brains.

As Jocko Willink explains in his book *Extreme Ownership*, you are either an effective leader or you're not. You either create value for your team, or you destroy it. There is no neutral. An effective leader is someone who sends people home feeling less stressed than when they came in and whose team members perform to the best of their capabilities. You either do that for your team, or you don't.

How do you know if you are an effective leader? Ask yourself: Would *all* your team members say you are someone who deliberately and intentionally sends everyone home without stress and feeling like they left nothing on the table today? Would *all* your team members say they feel free to be their true, authentic selves and are comfortable speaking up to anyone in the team about what's important to them?

When it comes to how you interact, influence, and lead others, pay attention to what people do and say about *you*. Are they enthused and inspired to work with you, or are they secretly cruising LinkedIn, looking to get the hell out of Dodge? Do people speak positively about you when you're not in the room? Do people actively *want* to work for and with you?

If the answer's no and you don't care about what your team thinks of you, that's a sure sign this book is for you and you need to CARE more about what's going on with your team.

In today's turbulent and unpredictable times with team members often working in remote locations, strong, effective leadership is paramount. The pandemic opened a chasm wider than the Grand Canyon between mediocrity and greatness. You must be more deliberate and intentional in how you lead now. You must use your time, which is a very finite resource when you're in leadership, as wisely as possible. You need to make time your friend, not your enemy. There is no hiding behind the energy and camaraderie of a bustling workplace. Every decision and action, or inaction, you make is glaringly obvious.

As leaders, we often need accurate "data" gained through honest feedback and candid conversations—the human skills every leader needs to have—to combat our internal programming and work toward being better versions of ourselves. We need to know whether we are leading effectively—not just from our *own point of view*, but from the POVs of those we serve.

> **Those we serve hold the keys to our effectiveness as leaders.**

Those we serve hold the keys to our effectiveness as leaders. If they feel safe enough to share these keys with us, they will. If they do not feel safe, they won't. Period. That is why psychological safety is such an important aspect of leadership and higher performance. It is the heart and soul of the CARE Equation and how you CARE to Win. Building our teams' psychological safety will help us break our biases and get to higher performance so everyone, not just one person, wins.

Psychological Safety and the Death of Silence and Stress

So, what exactly is psychological safety? Amy Edmondson, a top researcher on the subject, explains in her book *The Fearless Organization* that psychological safety is " . . . a shared belief held by members of a team that the team is safe for interpersonal risk-taking." If you're interested in investing in psychological safety (and you should be), please read it.

Let's focus on that last idea: risk-taking. Risk-taking entails speaking up, weighing in, and offering your ideas to the team. In most organizations, there is far too much silence. By that I don't mean mindful or meditative silence, I mean people failing to say what they're thinking out of fear of repercussions. Silence kills organizations. Silence kills leadership. Silence kills relationships.

Too many people go home to their families wishing they could have said something at work but didn't feel safe enough to speak up. They end up stressing about their inaction at home, which takes away from being fully present for their families.

Think about marriage. When couples only talk about the good things and don't speak up about the stuff that bothers them, they end up getting divorced. In the workplace, team members leaving or being actively disengaged is a "divorce." You can't be successful without a seasoned team behind you, and teams are solidified through psychological safety. That's how true performance comes out. Not from intimidation, threats, demands, or faulty assumptions that lead to bad decisions. And definitely not through silence.

As leaders, we need people to speak up. We need them to tell us what is working, so we do more of it. We need them to tell us what is not working, so we do less of it. It's that simple. That is the secret sauce of a high-performing team: everyone feels that when they speak up, they will be listened to and are valued for voicing their wants and needs. But they won't speak up unless they feel safe enough to do so. The importance of this cannot be overstated.

Group members will risk being authentic and vulnerable *only* when they believe they won't be penalized, rejected, or ridiculed for showing up as their true selves, being honest, speaking up, and making mistakes. This is where psychological safety is critical. It's the key ingredient to unleashing human potential, in work and in life.

Think of a team you are a part of. In that group, do you feel comfortable speaking up to everyone about tough issues without fear of what will happen if/when you do? Do you ever go home wishing you had said something, but you didn't because you didn't know how everyone would react? If this is how you feel on your team, or how you sense other people are feeling when they leave the office or come in, you might not have the type of psychological safety needed to be high performing.

How to tell if you do? Here are a few habits a high-performing, psychologically safe team share:

- Everyone feels free to share their thoughts without the perceived risk of repercussions. People are able to express their concerns openly to leaders and coworkers.
- The team leader sets an example by demonstrating behaviors conducive to psychological safety and others are expected to follow suit.
- People feel safe taking calculated risks. Everything becomes a possibility, and innovative ideas flow freely.
- People feel free to be the same person at work that they are at home.
- Innovation and creative solutions are applauded and rewarded.

Psychological safety, however, is *not* a scenario where employees and leaders:

- Share the first thing that comes into their minds.
- Remove all emotional and verbal filters.
- "Democratize" decision-making.
- Create a nice, fluffy environment where no one gets their feelings hurt.
- Try every idea presented and hope things work out.
- Tolerate everything and everyone, including bad decisions.
- Withhold feedback for fear of offending.
- Try to eliminate conflict or avoid hard conversations.

In a psychologically safe environment, people do not stay silent out of fear of negative consequences. Remember: silence kills leadership. We need our teams to speak up about what is working for them about our leadership performance, so we can do more of it. We need our teams to speak up about what is *not* working for them about our leadership performance, so we can do less of it.

If you're thinking this is all feel-good mumbo jumbo, think again. Google performed a study called Project Aristotle which revealed that psychological safety is the number one predictor of team effectiveness. Not two or three. Number *one*. It's the key to unlocking performance and well-being in teams.

Threat Detection

When psychological safety is present, team members feel safe to brainstorm without fear. They speak up and ask clarifying questions, maybe even challenge the status quo. They say what's on their mind versus holding back their truth when it matters. They can work to their fullest potential without fear. You can expect to see improved collaboration and innovation. You can also expect to see faster solutions to problems because employees feel safer reporting things that aren't working right, thus averting many crises before they even happen. In addition, psychological safety leads to lower workplace stress and increased job satisfaction.

Psychological safety creates an inclusive environment where people have a sense of belonging and feel free to be their true, authentic selves. Work becomes a safe space where good talent is curated, nurtured, and retained. You don't lose good employees to other opportunities; team members are invested in building something together.

And you have the key to build psychological safety and a winning team in your hand. It's called *CARE to Win*, which is all about giving you the keys to CARE so you can build psychological safety within your team and help you and your people feel like they are winning every single day.

Get to Psychological Safety with CARE

To achieve psychological safety, a team must CARE for one another. CARE is achieved through Clarity, Autonomy, Relationships, and Equity.

SAFE

UNSAFE

Performance Response

Survival Response

- **Clarity:** Team members feel they are all on the same line of the same page of the same book as one another. Their expectations are crystal clear. There is little to no ambiguity.
- **Autonomy:** Teams feel they are in control of their work and have freedom to make decisions. They can map out their own method of executing goals and achieve those goals in their own way, without being micromanaged.
- **Relationships:** Team members feel valued for who they are and what they bring to the team. The relational guards are down, and they don't feel like they're bound to working in silos.
- **Equity:** Resources and attention are allotted to those that need it most *when* they need it most, allowing a sense of fairness to pervade the team and workplace.

This is what I mean by CARE, but even the word "care" alone, without the embedded acronym, is a goal worth striving for. Care, as a noun, means that serious attention or consideration is being given so people avoid risks or damage. As a verb, it is protecting and providing what is necessary for the well-being of others. While the word might be something you hear a lot, that doesn't mean it's something to scoff at.

Caring for someone means we attach importance to them. We consciously strive not to cause them any harm or damage, and their needs and well-being become a high priority to us. Caring is not *self-centered* and *me-focused*. It is *self-less* and *we-focused*. It forces us to tell our biased brain no, get out of self-preservation mode, and put the wants and needs of others at the forefront. Leadership is about serving others—not about wielding power or authority over them. Just as we care for friends and family members, we should care for those we interact with on a day-to-day basis, especially those we lead.

Clarity + Autonomy + Relationships + Equity = CARE. By consistently providing CARE to those you serve, you understand that a team is more likely to feel safe when they can be their authentic selves, contribute, speak up, and offer their best work. High-performing teams need a high-performing leader (or leaders) who care. A leader who cares effectively builds psychological safety. When a team moves closer to being psychologically safe, they speak up about what is working, so they do more of it. They also speak up about what is not working, so the team does less of it. When the team speaks up, they're helping you ensure the longevity of the team and your influence as a leader. They help you be aware of how your team is doing and feeling instead of relying on your internal biases to tell you what's going on—which will more often be self-serving for your own ego and self-preservation instinct rather than serving the whole team. We all CARE to Win together.

Clarity + Autonomy + Relationships + Equity = CARE

To lead with CARE, you will need to keep your ego at bay. Lock it up. Ego is the enemy of self-awareness and selfless leadership. Ego keeps us stuck in our biases and tells us that feedback is unimportant, that we know what we're doing. CARE requires humility, vulnerability, and an acknowledgement of loss. If you have never lost at anything, or experienced any hardship, how on earth can you be humble? Everyone has failed or had unwanted results. The question is, did they admit it as their own failure or blame someone or something else? Humility brought about by loss is what triggers the growth mindset, and that's exactly the kind of mind needed to be a CAREing leader.

And that is what the CARE playbook is all about. CARE to Win is a mindset, not another model. It's the idea that you wake up with the right mindset that helps you to be intentional in how you communicate and collaborate with other people so they can be their best and do their best. That intentionality allows you to combat those biases and the ego we all have to build safe environments where both human and business performance thrive. When everyone feels like they are thriving, they'll be high-performing, and you'll know that you and your team are winning. Most importantly, your team will know that you CARE.

CHAPTER 2

HAVING THE RIGHT MINDSET TO
LEAD EFFECTIVELY

No one is born a leader. Leadership is learned. But anyone can *choose* to be a leader.

Leadership is like art, cooking, and golf—you can never perfect it. You can only continually improve upon it. As we talked about in Chapter 1, the brain has at least 188 cognitive biases, which means there are nearly two hundred potential blind spots to inhibit you from leading effectively. If the secret sauce of leadership is knowing and not assuming, and yet the brain is an assumption-making machine, then we have a built-in mountain to climb! Factoring in the huge challenge of shifting from a self-serving orientation to an other-serving orientation, this becomes a game not suited for casual climbers.

The first and most important step toward becoming a better leader is developing a *growth mindset* for leadership. A growth mindset entails a commitment to positive change, an understanding that change is a continual and unending process, a large dose of ego-killing humility, and a belief that you are capable of change.

The Growth Mindset

The term "growth mindset" was coined by author, psychologist, and Stanford University professor Dr. Carol Dweck in her book *Mindset: The New Psychology of Success.*[1] After decades of research, she discovered that the way students *perceived* their abilities played a huge role in their motivation and their level of achievement. According to Dr. Dweck, "Individuals who believe their talents can be developed (through hard work, good strategies, and input from others) have a growth mindset."[2]

In a TED Talk on the topic, Dr. Dweck discussed the growth mindset in the classroom.[3] Giving students a failing grade, she explained, was detrimental to their future success. By focusing on a grade or final test score, many students would develop a fear of failure. They would begin to define themselves by that next A or test score instead of focusing on what still needed to be learned or accomplished.

She told the story of a Chicago high school that adopted a new grading system. Students who were not doing passing work simply received a grade of "not yet," which allowed them to focus on those areas where they needed further instruction. The teacher began giving feedback on their *progress*, not their deficits, and rewarding them for *engagement in the process*. Dweck also described a kindergarten class whose test results soared to the top of the national charts after they were taught to embrace the *effort to learn* rather than the results.

What if that same philosophy was applied to your leadership? Instead of trying to prove what a great leader you already were, what if you could humble yourself enough to discover what you *don't* know yet and improve from there? No A grades. No certificates of completion. Just continual learning—like with art, cooking, and golf. Let go of the ego. Long live humility!

If you were convinced that you needed to change and *were able* to change, how much closer would you be to becoming the person and leader you really want to be?

The growth mindset requires an understanding that change is an unfolding process that never ends. Unlike the frazzled woman in the above illustration, growth-minded individuals never say, *I can't, I'll never, I am the way I am,* or speak in absolutes. They live by the mantra of "I am not there . . . *yet.*"

There is not a fixed destination for leadership, psychological safety, or high performance. You never will be there because the goal will always be evolving. You will never stop working toward a win because what you want to win will change. Even the best leaders, teammates, partners, coworkers—they *all* continuously strive to meet goals that are fluctuating month to month, week to week, and even day to day. Remember, "You are not there *yet*" means you have room for growth and change, as does your team. Growth takes time for everyone, and change is good. That means you can take the pressure off and start enjoying the ride. When you are present in the journey to win at work, you'll become a more CAREing leader.

Fixed Mindset vs. Growth Mindset

The opposite of a growth mindset is a fixed mindset.[4] In essence, this is the belief that your traits and capabilities are largely fixed and innate. It's the thinking that *"The amount of intelligence and talent I currently possess is the amount I will always have, so I'd better make the most of it."*

The fixed mindset has an intriguing corollary: you develop the compulsive need to be seen as perfect just the way you are. In one way or another, you're always proving yourself, demonstrating your skills, or trying to perform better than others. You want to get all A's, and you lose your sh*t when you get a B. A fixed mindset shapes the world into one big competition where you're either winning or losing. And losing is not an option to your ego-minded brain.

A fixed mindset is like putting a permanent lock on your capabilities. And along with the belief that you are not able to change comes a sneaking fear of *"What if I'm not good enough? I could make mistakes. Others may do it better."* You live in private dread of being "found out," so you work hard to make sure that never happens.

A fixed mindset hinders you from developing skills and talents that come with experience. For example, I have a fixed mindset for cooking. I truly believe I was born a terrible cook. Every time I cook, my brain plays tricks on me and tells me not to go off the recipe for fear of creating a culinary disaster. I am locked. My learning and ability to improve are hindered. And every mistake I make only reinforces my belief in my inability to cook. One year, I invited my team over for Thanksgiving dinner and put three tablespoons of baking powder into my sticky toffee pudding, not three teaspoons. The result was god-awful, and they will rib me about it for life. For me, that was further damning evidence that I don't belong in the same zip code as a kitchen.

Let's face it: not everyone can be great at everything. For statistics to work, there must be a median, and an equal number of people must rise above and fall below it. Only one of us was born Picasso, Tiger Woods, or Julia Child, but if you practiced as often as they did, you would be surprised by how much skill you're able to develop. And if you hired a good coach, you would improve even more. Virtually every skill can be improved upon. Just like leadership.

Nobody is born a leader. Leadership is a learned skill.

We come into this world relying on other people's help to survive. We require the guidance, wisdom, and knowledge of those around us to develop. This process does not stop, even when

> Nobody is born a leader. Leadership is a learned skill.

we become leaders of others. Leadership is a complex and multidimensional endeavor. We can always develop new skills to lead more efficiently and effectively.

It's a mistake to ever believe you're a "finished product." You may have gifts that come naturally to you, but if you believe that your one natural skill set is all a strong leader needs, then you're severely limiting your potential growth and effectiveness as a leader.

Most of us have a mixture of fixed and growth mindsets in different areas of our lives, and that's okay. There is nothing inherently wrong with deciding, for example, *I'll never be a great golfer,* and putting your efforts for growth elsewhere. We all need to choose our battles. But in any area that might be affecting the achievement of your long-term goals or your longevity and health, it is vital to switch to a growth mindset.

It's important to recognize, however, that the growth mindset doesn't imply an "I can do anything" attitude when it comes to trying new things. Without a little humility and a *lot* of learning, the growth-mindset recipe would be ineffective and taste just as bad as my aforementioned sticky toffee pudding.

The Dunning-Kruger Effect

You've probably been there: After firing up a couple of "Teach Yourself" videos on YouTube, you're ready to tackle a serious DIY project. You have all the confidence in the world—until step one ends up taking three hours instead of five minutes. You've dramatically underestimated how much time this kind of project takes and overestimated your skills.

We've all found ourselves, at some point in our careers and lives, biting off more than we can chew. Our confidence blinded our competence. In scientific circles, this is known as the Dunning-Kruger (DK) Effect: a cognitive bias whereby you think you can easily accomplish things you're not actually skilled at.

David Dunning and Justin Kruger—for whom the bias was named—were two social psychologists whose work was inspired by the profound failings of a gentleman named McArthur Wheeler. In 1995, Wheeler concocted a "perfect crime" after learning that lemon juice was an agent in disappearing ink.

Wheeler reasoned that since lemon juice could produce invisible writing, it would also render the human face invisible on security cameras. Quite the leap of logic, but not for McArthur Wheeler. Armed with confidence in his theory and, presumably, a weapon of some kind, he rubbed lemon juice on his face and proceeded to rob a Pittsburgh bank in broad daylight—even smiling for the cameras on his way out. He blithely went on to rob a *second* bank.

Unsurprisingly, he was apprehended by the police a short while later. During his arrest procedure, he was shown the video of his crime, in which his face was clearly visible. "But I wore the juice," he muttered incredulously.[5]

Dunning and Kruger were intrigued by the story. How could anyone have such misplaced assuredness in their own capabilities? So they decided to design a study. They asked students a series of questions covering several topic areas and then scored their answers. After, each participant was asked to guess their own score and to estimate how well they did compared to other test-takers. The researchers discovered that people in the bottom 25th percentile consistently ranked their abilities at higher than 70 percent, while those in the top percentile rated themselves lower than their actual ranking.[6] Why is this?

The answer lies at the heart of human growth. Essentially, people "don't know what they don't know." The depth of ignorance can be profound—as in the case of McArthur Wheeler—and often extends to an inability to recognize the difference between a good performance and a poor one. Incompetent people don't know how incompetent they are. So they don't seek out feedback, training, and knowledge. They tend to rely on a quick Google search, YouTube video, or TikTok, since that can *always* render them an "instant expert" on anything (or so they think).

What is it that hinders people's ability to recognize their own incompetency? Why do so many leaders think they are the most amazing leaders ever, yet their teams think they suck? Simple: they lack humility. People who are low performers are often poor at accepting criticism and show little interest in self-improvement. In other words, they have a fixed mindset.

By contrast, the top scorers in the DK Effect study rated themselves at a lower level because high performers typically have the self-awareness to recognize their own deficits. Because of this, they are motivated to learn so they can correct those deficits. This motivated learning, in turn, produces higher levels of competency, which explains the higher test scores. This is the growth mindset at work.

Growth-minded people are aware of their limitations, which allows them to work on expanding them. Fixed-minded people fail to see their own limitations; therefore, no growth needed!

DK Effect Alexample

I received my first major dose of the Dunning-Kruger Effect in high school. In the UK, where I grew up before moving to the states in 2005, students are required to select their A-levels at the age of sixteen. These are subject areas of advanced concentration, similar to AP courses in the US (we specialize early in Britain). By the time I was sixteen, I had already been a cadet in the Royal Air Force, I had traveled to Germany to spend time at a base, and I'd flown single-prop trainer planes. I'd made my big choice in life: I was going to be a fighter pilot. I was brimming with unearned confidence simply because my flight trainer had told me a few times I was "great." I felt invincible!

Out of the dozen-plus courses, I picked math, physics, and geography to be my A-level concentrations. And to become a pilot, I also needed to get As in math and physics. Not my strongest subjects. But my cockiness told me I could easily improve in both subjects. *"How difficult can it be?"* was my attitude. Without sufficient forethought, and without seeking anyone else's perspective, I chose to wing it through two subjects I was clearly not going to master any time soon.

It didn't take long to realize the enormous challenge involved in earning an A in both math and physics. I ended up failing, and it took me many years to get back on the right road.

The DK Effect in Business

In my work as a leadership trainer, I see the Dunning-Kruger Effect in action over and over again. Often, when business leaders are promoted to their first leadership position, they assume their promotion is a testament to their competence. They then set forth to prove to everyone that they know what they're doing. They don't ask what their team needs from them, and they don't ask the experts around them for advice. Rather, they try to run everything themselves.

Instead of humility, they choose hubris and root themselves in ignorance.

The brain is designed to make assumptions to increase the changes of your survival, but sometimes this can set you up for failure as a leader unless you challenge those assumptions. How do you do that? By relentlessly asking *questions*.

Yes, it's that simple. And that tricky.

I could have spared myself my traumatic high school experience, and the ensuing setback in my life, had I only slowed down, asked more questions, and not made assumptions. *All* my life's failures, in fact, could have been prevented or mitigated by this one practice. Perhaps the same is true for you.

Ego is the death of good leadership. How do you reduce ego? By being curious and humble enough to ask questions and shift your perspective. How do you trigger the growth mindset? By questioning your competence in every area.

> # Ego is the death of good leadership.

Competence flows from failure

Failure is the world's greatest teacher. Competence is the product of learning from past failures. So how can you gain competence if you don't acknowledge failure? The most growth-minded people are unafraid to look their failures squarely in the eye and own them. They know that every failure contains a goldmine of information on what to do *right*. They don't dwell on past failures. Rather, they acknowledge the failure, mine it for its gold, and then move on.

Confidence is equally important

At the same time, everyone needs competence and confidence. We need the competence to know what decisions to make, and confidence is essential to know we're making the right decision at the right time, regardless of the outcome. This comes from a balance of acknowledging failure and embracing success.

If you endure too much failure without experiencing success, your brain will eventually revolt and go into a negative spiral. Therefore, we must celebrate successes, regardless of their magnitude. Someone who goes through too many failures without acknowledging any successes they have may lose their belief in themselves to the point where they start to experience imposter syndrome.

On the other hand, too many perceived successes without an acknowledgement of failure tends to stimulate the Dunning-Kruger Effect. A big part of leadership is knowing how to strike this balance—both with the people we lead and with ourselves.

Self-Awareness

In order to stay humble, you must begin to acknowledge what you don't know and take active steps to develop the skills you're lacking. This involves seeking feedback and criticism. At the same time, you must also give yourself credit for the strengths and skills you possess. If you don't believe in yourself, you will second-guess every decision you make. Again, it's all about balance.

This balance is called self-awareness, and it's the secret sauce to that fine line between humility and confidence. Self-awareness is an ability to see yourself with a measure of objectivity and to critically observe your thoughts, emotions, and motivations.

Five ways to support your self-awareness

Self-awareness is an ongoing growth process that includes taking the following steps:

1. **Ask yourself "Why?" many times a day.** Develop a habit of continually asking, "Why do I think that? Why is that my conclusion? Why do I trust this 'data'?" Self-aware people are open to challenging themselves because they believe in the process of critical thinking. Ask "Why?" even more than a four-year-old does.

2. **Trace your assumptions.** Whenever you make a declarative statement of "fact" ("That's the way things are," "This is the best course of action," "This is what we should do . . ."), trace

your reasoning back as far as you can. When did you first come to this conclusion? Evaluate the objectivity of your platform.

3. **Own your strengths and weaknesses.** What comes easier to you than to others? What have you struggled with more than others have? Learn to leverage your strengths wherever you can, but also strive to be conscious of your weaknesses. Often your biggest strength can be your biggest weakness in a different context, so become aware of your habits. Increase those that build your strengths and decrease those that play to your weaknesses.

4. **Work on your metacognition.** Make *metacognition* (developing awareness and understanding of your own thought process) a regular exercise. Step back from your day-to-day thinking and look at the big picture of who you are and what you're up to. Journal, meditate, exercise, or go to coaching or therapy. Shift your perspective.

5. **Develop a network of trusted peers.** Put some time and effort into figuring out whose opinions you trust and keep those people close. Develop candid relationships where you can trust that their criticism is constructive and ask for their feedback often.

All of these ways to become self-aware are amplified by the process of reflection. When you reflect on past experiences, relationships, values, beliefs, and actions, we automatically get curious and ask ourselves lots of questions to try to shift our perspective and challenge any assumptions our brain has made. Here are some scenarios and reflection questions that can support the above steps to becoming more self-aware:

1. You are presenting a project that you feel confident in to a peer or team member you're in charge of. They give you some feedback about the process, and while you thank them for it, you don't implement it when you go back to work on the project some more. Ask yourself: *Why did you dismiss their input?* Then ask: *Why did they give that specific feedback? Would you react the same way, or implement their feedback, knowing what you know now? Why or why not?*

2. Think of an assumption you might have. Maybe it's that morning meetings work best for everyone because we haven't looked at our emails and have more mental capacity to give to the meeting. Now, ask yourself: *Is this belief realistic? Is it supported by evidence? Do you feel defensive when someone (directly or indirectly) questions your call for having only morning meetings or whatever area you have a lot of knowledge in? Would you be willing to have everyone you know critique your reasoning for why morning meetings are the only way to do meetings? Why or why not?*

3. You are sitting down with your boss for your annual review, and beforehand, you have to fill out a few questions about what you think your strengths are. You are also asked to fill out weaknesses that you have and want to improve. *What are the key traits, talents, and strengths upon which you build your self-image? What do you believe you're really good at? Is it important for you to be the best at this? Why? Are there any areas of life or business where you can admit to possibly knowing less than you assume yourself to know? Where do you want to grow but don't know how to start?* This is something you should address with your boss in that meeting.

4. You used to do your favorite activity every single day before you got promoted. Maybe it was running, reading, or painting. It gave you time to think and ask yourself what you wanted in order to get this promotion. *Do you miss that activity? How have you been performing since dropping it off your plate? Do you feel better, worse, the same? If you feel worse, what are ways you can delegate to your team to make more time to take care of you?*

5. You're a week away from delivering your presentation on a major project to your boss but want some feedback before the day. *Who are you asking when you need advice? Is it an expert, a friend, a general work colleague? Have you developed relationships with these people that will give you the honest feedback you need to succeed? Is their feedback helpful and will it make you come out feeling more or less prepared?*

Leaders Who CARE to Win
Have a Growth Mindset

The reason my team has done so much research on cognitive biases is to help you see that we all, from time to time, can be a**holes. That includes the best leaders I know. No one's above this, and everyone falls to it. I've done it. And I'm pretty sure it's happened to you too. Like our biases, it's human nature, and those same biases can prevent us from seeing this and keep us from becoming the leaders we were meant to be. My hope is that in pointing out these biases, just as we did with the Dunning-Kruger Effect, and encouraging a growth mindset, you will be better able to understand how your mind operates. Simply by being aware of each bias and watching how it shows up in your life, you will become a more evolved leader. Again, we don't know what we don't know. And trust me, we don't know a lot!

The goal of the CARE Equation is to help you break your bad habits (or biases) and learn how to give your people what they need—not what *you* need. Two of the great discoveries of the modern leadership era are the importance of developing emotional intelligence and the need to create a psychologically safe workspace for your team members. Understanding CARE combines both and will help you develop teams that feel empowered to speak their mind, innovate, collaborate, and stay in the game. This is the key to fostering high performance while also developing a more humane and enjoyable workplace.

As we move through the book, we will dig into each component of the CARE Equation and then in two main cognitive biases in that area. But to really learn the playbook and put it into practice, you must actively apply your new knowledge. In Malcolm Gladwell's popular book *Outliers*, he says it takes ten thousand hours of deliberate practice to achieve mastery.[7] To help you get started on those hours, there are exercises along the way so you can see how these biases show up in your life and you can learn how to overcome them. Be prepared to do the work! This will lead you to success faster than anything else.

The purpose of this chapter was to show you the *why*. To give you context. To get your brain ready for the tough lessons ahead. Now, if you are ready, let's get to the heart of what it means to grow yourself into a self-aware leader who can build psychological safety for your team and organization, outperform your peers, and show those you lead that you CARE to Win.

PART I

Clarity

Autonomy

Relationships

Equity

CHAPTER 3

THE IMPORTANCE OF
CLARITY

I spent twenty-two years developing and delivering in-person leadership experiences (i.e., I would put myself or my trainers in the same room with the trainees). For the five years leading up to the COVID-19 pandemic, DX Learning had used only this in-person model. To me, there didn't seem to be any other way to do the kind of work we do. Changing behavior for the better meant we *had* to get people together in the same room. It was a no-brainer.

Or maybe not.

On March 6, 2020, just before all hell broke loose, I was about to board a plane to Los Angeles to deliver a keynote address at a conference. Up to that point, I held the belief, like so many others, that COVID was just a bad flu-like illness and would soon blow over. Just as I stepped up to hand my ticket to the gate agent, I received a call. Without even answering it, I instinctively knew: the event had been canceled. I headed back to the lounge area, grabbed a glass of wine, and began to prepare myself for what might happen next.

Later that afternoon, a second large event was canceled, and then another, and another. The hopelessness of the situation started to grab hold of me. I felt sick to my stomach. Cold sweats. It was like when you go to a large event with your children and look round, and one of them is missing. That "oh shit" feeling. I will never forget it.

Live events were my company's bread and butter—its sole source of income. So I spent that weekend reflecting and gaining clarity. I had to slow my brain down, gather data, and do some serious introspection to prepare myself and my team for the cliff's edge we were heading straight toward—and which we had no control over. It was definitely a time to be CAREful, not CAREless. Providing Clarity to my team was the first and only step I could take.

On March 9, I walked into the office, knowing we had about a four-week time frame to drastically change our business model, as everything we'd been doing would soon be rendered obsolete. I knew I had to state the unvarnished truth: if we didn't move quickly and find new solutions before the world shut down, I couldn't guarantee the team's jobs or security. I was brutally honest, but I hoped if we could quickly bring a virtual product to market, our company might have a fighting chance.

I didn't have all the answers, but I believed that with the team's help, feedback, and creativity, we could create something to replace our in-person training model.

We asked each other a lot of questions. What did we know? What didn't we know? What did we need to get done? How long did we have? Who needed to do what? And we relentlessly thrashed out the answers.

Coming from a place of honesty, transparency, and vulnerability, I sought to provide the team the Clarity they needed to step up to the plate. We arrived at a shared set of crystal-clear expectations, which led to a set of collective goals. We were all on the same page. It wasn't a *good* page, but at least we were all on it.

Over the next three weeks, all revenue ceased as the world shut down. But by April, because we had come together with Clarity as a team, we were able to quickly bring a virtual product to the marketplace to replace our in-person-events style of training. It's amazing what a team can do when it's galvanized by Clarity as opposed to fighting ambiguity. Our company is still around and thriving today.

> It's amazing what a team can do when it's galvanized by Clarity as opposed to fighting ambiguity.

Defining Clarity

You know the feeling. You've just had a conversation with someone, and you walk away with a sense of "*I think I know what they mean, but I am not entirely sure.*" Or you attend a meeting where a high-level person makes a statement no one understands. You can see the look of confusion on everyone's faces, but no one dares say anything. Maybe you've sat with a doctor as they explained a medical condition to you, but much of it went over your head. You ran home to google the medical terms only to work yourself into an even bigger frenzy or discover there was nothing to worry about—but that period of anxiety sure robbed your peace of mind for a while. You lacked Clarity, and you filled in the blanks with fear.

It's a bad feeling when you're not on the same page with someone important, or even worse, when you *thought* you were on the same page, only to find out days or weeks later you were reading different books entirely! Business decisions, and life decisions, often go off the rails when Clarity is absent.

In terms of leadership, Clarity can be defined as *a shared understanding of crystal-clear expectations to achieve collective goals.*

Sounds simple enough. Then why is Clarity so elusive? Why is it we don't seek Clarity all the time?

The short answer? Fear.

Fear Foils Clarity

Our brain is like a series of maps. These maps capture our experiences and memories, then provide a way for us to interpret and categorize new information. When information is presented to us that does not align with these maps, ambiguity arises. If the information is potentially life-affecting, our threat circuitry activates. The limbic system—the primitive, self-protective, survival-driven part of the brain—kicks in. We go into fight-or-flight mode.

The brain does not like unfamiliarity. It does not like the unknown. The unknown is stressful and creates fear.

When faced with ambiguity, your instinct is to try to resolve the uncertainty. You want to say something, but you may not feel safe enough to do so. The cognitive stress on the brain caused by the perceived threat of the unknown inhibits your ability to be your natural self. You don't want to take a risk by asking the question you know you need to ask. Your brain tells you that if you say something, you're going to look like an idiot, or you're going to trigger some other negative consequence, and so you *say nothing*! You opt for silence.

Silence kills business.

Silence kills leadership.

Silence kills relationships.

Remember, the number one purpose of the brain is to keep us alive. In addition to our reptilian brain (limbic system), which is essentially our fight-or-flight instinct, the higher brain (the neocortex) is a prediction machine, and it is always trying to ensure that what's in our world is familiar. If something is *un*familiar, this lack of security can unleash the *negativity bias* (among other biases, as we'll soon see). This is a tendency of human beings to allow negative news, events, or possibilities to affect us more powerfully than positive things. Simply put, when we encounter situations of uncertainty, we tend to gravitate more to worry and unease than eager anticipation. Like when a leader tells the team, "Next quarter will be challenging." Each team member believes their job is in jeopardy. When we don't know something, we fill in the blanks with negative news.

A sense of certainty, on the other hand, creates cognitive ease. Without cognitive ease, cortisol—the stress hormone—is released, and we go into threat-avoidance mode. This saps power from the decision-making part of the brain, and we can't function at our optimal level. Fear literally shuts down our higher thinking capacities. Clarity, however, removes ambiguity, which in turn alleviates fear and allows our brains to work at a higher level.

Humans have craved Clarity since our species' origin because we need it to survive. We needed to know where it was safe to eat and drink. We needed to know who was on saber-toothed tiger watch on a given night. If we weren't certain, it could mean death.

The brain still views uncertainty as a threat today. Though we have swapped out saber-toothed tigers for bosses, cars, and deadly viruses, the brain is still a survival machine. It still craves Clarity. That's what helps it survive. We need to help our teams feel psychologically safe and at cognitive ease. We do this by ensuring they have enough Clarity.

Clarity in Communication and Leadership

According to research in a *Forbes* article, 86 percent of employees blame lack of good communication for workplace failures.[1] Conversely, *good* communication is the best predictor of high employee engagement.[2] How do you think this information might apply to your team or your employees?

Effective communication goes a long way toward eliminating ambiguity. And by effective communication, I mean two-way communication. With *meaningful* back-and-forth.

Communication is not a one-time message sent out along a one-way avenue. Many unenlightened leaders think that simply by issuing an edict "from above"—for example, a memo stating, "From now on, all team leaders will submit evaluation reports on a monthly basis."—they can effectively initiate change in their organization. But the response to such unilateral communication is usually resistance or confusion. Team members wonder: *Which level of team leader do they mean? Evaluation of what? Submit to whom? Why? Is this important, or is it something I can just ignore for now?*

When Clarity is missing from communication, there is ample room for error and failure, and teams have difficulty reaching collective goals together. Team members approach their tasks in a state of ambiguity. Does the brain like ambiguity? Not at all. It sees ambiguity as a threat. And so, anxiety prevails. The brain is compromised, which makes the team, and the organization's overall mission, compromised.

Why do we so often communicate poorly? Bad assumptions. Remember, the brain is an assumption-making machine. It assumes everyone somehow has access to our thoughts (we'll talk about this bias in the next chapter), and it gets annoyed when others don't know what we are thinking. We assume that by saying something just once, or even by failing to communicate it at all, everyone will be aligned and on the same page. The actual result is that people come to work not knowing what they are supposed to be doing or why, when, and how.

This is especially problematic when the company faces a crisis. That's the time when efficient, focused, coordinated action is essential. Clearly defined goals and expectations can make the difference between a company surviving a disaster or going under because of it.

It is crucial for your team to have a shared understanding of where things stand and what you're doing. When you create Clarity together, you are likely to be on the same page and have crystal-clear expectations the first time around. With crystal-clear expectations, you can achieve collective goals. This entails a "we" mentality, not an "I" mentality.

An open and dynamic two-way exchange allows misunderstandings to be resolved and Clarity to be attained. Good communicators always keep the communication loop in mind.

The communication loop

No communication can be considered complete until this loop is completed:

1. **The sender has a clear message they want to communicate.** Don't try to communicate until you know what you want to say. Don't waste people's mental bandwidth on ambiguous phrasing and filler speech.

2. **The sender encodes the message.** The sender puts their message into written, spoken, or visual language. Some of your original meaning is always lost at this point due to your heuristics and biases. (That's why communicating in multiple ways, multiple times, is essential.)

3. **The recipient decodes the message.** The recipient interprets what the sender is trying to communicate. They always do this through their own filter of heuristics and biases.

4. **The recipient gives the message back to the sender.** The recipient tells the sender, in one way or another, *"Here is what I heard you say."*

5. **The sender confirms that the recipient got it right or not.** If the recipient did not get it right or something was lost in translation, it's up to the sender to ask questions so they know what the recipient is thinking and what was lost while also encouraging the recipient to ask their own questions of the sender. Questions like "What did I miss?" or "What parts of the material aren't making sense?" and "How can we get more aligned on this topic?" Once the sender and recipient are on the same page, the loop restarts.

Clarity is achieved by using this two-way communication approach. Good communicators internalize the communication loop and use it habitually. They are confident but humble and unafraid to ask and answer questions. They constantly check to make sure their message has been received, acknowledge the feedback given by their team, and incorporate it to refine their message in a meaningful way that furthers communication. They seek feedback from the team and use the team's input to change or reshape the message. They observe their team's reactions and behavior to see if it indicates complete understanding or, if not, they follow up to make sure there are no assumptions so that everyone is on the same line of the same page.

The key is to ensure that your team has the information they need to move forward confidently. Verify that there is shared understanding by questioning your team and letting them feel safe enough to tell you if there isn't. Always ask people to repeat back, in their own words, what they've heard. That's the only way to ensure everyone is on the same line of the same page and not on different chapters (or even in a different book).

Writing things down is essential too; it allows people a chance to see it in black and white and give feedback. On our team, we notice that people feel safer to speak up when they can see things in written or graphic form. For example, we write the goals for the year on a large whiteboard as well as how we are doing versus what we've promised to do. For those not in the office, we send the visual update every Monday. It's easier for the brain to process visual information than information presented only verbally. Visual information also feels less personal than spoken information, so people feel freer to comment on it and offer critical feedback.

Everyone must "buy the why"

In order to attain high performance, your team must have collective goals. And when it comes to a collective goal, everyone must have Clarity on the "Why" behind what they are doing so they can move forward together synchronously to achieve it.

Simon Sinek's book, *Start with Why*, asserts that if you want to be an inspirational leader, you must start by identifying your purpose, cause, or vision. The "Why" is at the center of everything you do and must be fully understood and endorsed by the whole team. Only when the team has Clarity on the "Why" can you move outward to the "How" (the actions needed to realize the "Why") and then to the "What" (the product or end result the team wants to create).[3]

The "Why" stems from your core purpose. If your team has a clear understanding of this core purpose, there will be much more Clarity in executing the "What" and the "How." As Sinek explains, "People don't buy what you do, they buy why you do it."[4] A huge part of a leader's role is to constantly bring Clarity to the whole process: here's *why* we are doing this, here's *how* we will accomplish it, and here is *what* we need to produce to make it all work.

Let's ask what you can do with your own team to bring more Clarity right now.

START-STOP-CONTINUE EXERCISE

Ask yourself these start-stop-continue questions:

Start—*What am I not doing that I need to* start *doing, to bring more Clarity to my team? Who is not getting the message fully? Why? What can I do to change that?*

Stop—*What am I currently doing that I need to* stop *doing, to bring more Clarity to my team? What bad habits have I fallen into that obscure the message? How am I muddying things up? In what areas am I trying to know or do too much?*

Continue—*What am I currently doing that is creating positive Clarity for my team and that I should* continue *doing? What's working right now? How do I know?*

Questions you could ask *your* boss are just as important. *Your* brain also needs Clarity, so you can pass on more Clarity to those you serve.

Start—*What is my boss not doing that they need to* start *doing, to bring more Clarity to me and my team?*

Stop—*What is my boss currently doing that they need to* stop *doing, to bring more Clarity to me and my team?*

Continue—*What is my boss currently doing that is creating positive Clarity for me and my team and that they should* continue *doing?*

Now that you know how important Clarity is to effective leadership and its connection to psychological safety, it's time to look at some biases that can get in your way of achieving it. The next two chapters will present two common mental blind-spots that trap us all from time to time. More importantly, they will offer you some ways to *beat* those biases in order to become the Clarity-providing leader your team craves.

CHAPTER 4

CLARITY BIAS #1
THE CURSE OF KNOWLEDGE

Imagine that you're sitting with a doctor, engineer, or other professional, and they're explaining a "simple" concept to you. They immediately start making shorthand references to facts and principles you don't understand, and before long, you're hopelessly lost. They assume *their* pool of scientific or technical knowledge is shared by you—and by everyone else.

Or maybe someone (like, oh let's say, your mother) is telling you a story, and they immediately start referring to people and events you've never heard of. Somehow, they assume that because *they* know who their friends and neighbors are, you automatically know too.

These are everyday examples of the Curse of Knowledge Bias, or what we might call the *context fallacy*. This bias creates a daily challenge for us all and causes much unnecessary stress.

The Curse of Knowledge

One of my biggest challenges is that I have been in the leadership training industry since 2002. Often, I assume my team, my clients, and the people I interact with have the same level of experience and the same general background and knowledge that I have. Sometimes I'll explain something briefly and then jump to the next thing, assuming they understood what on earth I was talking about. They nod their heads and smile as if they get it (see Chapter 3), and I confidently continue moving on. Of course, they *didn't* get it, and that lack of Clarity comes back to bite me later.

The bias: When communicating with others, we tend to overestimate how much of our private context they understand. The more knowledge we have in an area, the more "cursed" by that knowledge we tend to be.

The effect on Clarity: We think and assume people are on the same page as us but often they're not.

The cure: *Stop* assuming that what is understood by you is understood by others. *Start* ensuring you are on the same page as the person you are communicating with.

The Curse of Knowledge Alexample

As an entrepreneur, my brain is wired for speed. If I don't take the time to slow down, I often find myself having to redo emails or reschedule meetings because I wrongly assumed everyone was on the same page with me.

One time, I got this so totally wrong when my company, DX, was going through a big branding overhaul. Our thinking was that if we wanted to compete with the big names in our industry, we needed to look the part. We spent a lot of money and time creating a new brand. After six months of hard work, we were getting close to finalizing it, but all the work had been done *internally*, within our team and our agency. We didn't know how our new ideas were going to fly with the outside world. I decided (emphasis on "I") that we should get a group of our local clients together in Chicago to solicit their feedback before we pulled the trigger.

In a meeting with my marketing coordinator, I explained my plan. "How about, in a few weeks, we get our clients to come to the office together, check out our brand, give us feedback on what they see?" Their reply was, "Great idea!"

What assumptions were being made here? *Which clients? Which brand, the new or the old? How will people give us feedback? What does a "few weeks" mean?* The idea in *my* head was to contact a few of DX's biggest fans from the Chicago area, get them in a room with some wine and cheese (you know, the classy thing to do), and show them a few pictures of the new brand to see what they thought. I wanted to see the looks on their faces to get a feel for how it resonated with our target audiences.

But what the marketing coordinator heard was, "Let's get *all* our clients in the Midwest together for a black-tie event where we will do a huge reveal of the finished brand (which we haven't finished yet and are working feverishly to complete)." She didn't sleep much for the next week. When I saw how stressed she was, I took her aside and discovered we were not on the same page. At all. We were in different books, and we certainly did not have Clarity.

Due to my own bias, I had caused unneeded stress in the life of someone important to me. Because of that stress, she was afraid to speak up. She did not ask questions. Once we got on the same page, she was relieved, to say the least, and the end result was a stellar event. The office was packed full of people we trusted and treasured the opinion of and who let us know their thoughts on our new brand which allowed us to polish it off into what you see today. If I had not checked in and checked my bias, the end of the story would not have been all smiles.

Silence kills business. Silence kills relationships.

Knowledge and Experience Play Into the "Curse"

The more experienced you are at something, the more likely this bias will catch you off guard.

We all tend to fill in the gaps in a story or a plan with our own knowledge. The more experience and knowledge we have, the more details we unconsciously fill in. For example, if I tell you about a dream I had, I may believe I'm painting an accurate picture. That's because I'm filling in all the unspoken gaps with my own experience and memory. You do not have the same images or memories to pull from, so you fill in those gaps with your own details. The result? Same description, different inner experiences. Not the same page, not even the same book.

Books are, in fact, another good example of this phenomenon. How many times have you read a novel and then seen the adapted movie, only to be disappointed that it didn't match your vision at all? Why didn't it? Because the screenwriter, director, set designer, and casting director all filled in the unwritten gaps with their own mental details. They saw the same story differently from their unique pools of knowledge and experience.

It is impossible for our brains to transfer the full cognitive load of information we carry to another person. To do so, we would need to have full conscious awareness of all our *own* knowledge as well as all that of the *other* person. The best we can do is establish some common knowledge and use that as a basis for communication. Gaps are inevitable, and where there are gaps, everyone fills them in based on their own context. This often leads to misunderstandings and frustrating situations.

Have you ever done a work presentation where you had a great vision and a perfect plan of execution, but your management team rejected the proposal simply because they didn't "see" it? The management received the Curse of Knowledge which triggered fear and rejection. What was great in your eyes was not great in theirs. Or maybe you've been in a classroom and your brilliant instructor had difficulty teaching the subject because they could no longer remember what it felt like to be a new student learning the subject for the first time? The instructor is cursed, and you received their instructions but not in a way that made sense to you, causing ambiguity and fear. Something as simple as a calendar invite to your team may need to be clarified, even if it makes perfect sense to you. And if it's being sent to people outside your team, it may need to be clarified even further. Your team's jargon and verbal shorthand might mean something entirely different to someone else. That someone else might see that jargon as threatening, as they don't know and feel like they should.

When we are on the receiving end of the Curse of Knowledge, we have to waste energy, time, and resources filling in the knowledge gaps. This stresses the brain out, which triggers the threat circuitry and lowers trust levels. But remember: high performance occurs only when *everyone* is on the same line of the same page.

Think of a time when you were on the receiving end of the Curse of Knowledge. What was the impact? One time that stands out for me is when I was making the decision to bring a retirement plan for all the DX team members. I remember my financial advisor sending me an email with the three options and a lot of acronyms and financial jargon that accompanied those three options. Of course, this was all super clear to them, as I'm sure they have done this a few times before, but that email caused an immense amount of fear—fear of the unknown—in me. I reread it at least five times. I then asked a number of friends to help decipher some of the jargon. All of this diverted time and energy from other issues when I could've gone to the advisor directly and asked my questions or the advisor could've asked me if I had any questions about the plans and what the terms meant. What was simple for my advisor was not simple for me. Likewise, what is simple for you is not simple for others.

How the Bias Was Identified

In 1990, an experiment was run by a Stanford University graduate student, Elizabeth Newton. Test subjects were asked to "tap" out well-known songs with their fingers while other subjects tried to name the songs. When the "tappers" were asked to predict how many of the "tapped" songs would be recognized by their listeners, they guessed, on average, it would be about 50 percent. In reality, only 2.5 percent of the tunes were guessed by the listeners.[1]

The "tappers" were so familiar with what they were tapping—and had the benefit of being able to hear the notes in their heads—that they assumed listeners would easily recognize the tunes. There's the Curse of Knowledge on full display. All of us "tap tunes," so to speak, on a regular basis and assume others are hearing the symphonic melodies in our heads. I challenge you to tap a song to a friend or coworker today and see if they get it or not.

Unclear Knowledge Can Have Deadly Costs

The cost of this bias isn't just frustration among team members. Sometimes it can lead to more severe consequences, such as the loss of life. Recently, IKEA, famous for their wordless, graphics-driven instruction manuals, came under fire when several children were injured or killed by falling shelf-units, all due to a lack of anchoring straps. The installation of this component was drawn unclearly in the instructions. IKEA designers assumed the readers would get the picture. And why not? *They* understood it because *they* built these units every day.

> The more competent you are at something, the more likely you will omit key elements when communicating with others.

The Curse of Knowledge strikes again. The more competent you are at something, the more likely you will omit key elements when communicating with others. Examples abound of how one person's context differs from another's and how this can cause Clarity problems. Here are a few acronyms we use every day that can muck up the meaning of even a simple text or email:

LOL—Laugh Out Loud OR Lots of Love
EA—East Asia OR Electronic Arts OR Executive Assistant
POS—Point of Sale OR Piece of Sh*t
MAGA—Make America Great Again OR Mexican American Grocers Association
WW—Worldwide Wrestling Federation OR World Wildlife Fund
CBD—Christian Book Distributors OR Cannabidiol-dimethylheptyl
CIA—Culinary Institute of America OR Central Intelligence Agency
ATM—Automated Teller Machine OR At the Moment
POC—Point of Contact OR Person of Color
PA—Performance Appraisal OR Physician's Assistant
CPU—Central Processing Unit OR Cost per Unit
CTA—Call to Action OR Chicago Transit Authority

When people don't know what an acronym means, they often hesitate to seek clarification for fear of looking stupid or not being part of the "in" group that understands the jargon. Whenever you use acronyms to speed things up for yourself, ask yourself if you might be slowing things down for others and if they will need to decode what you meant.

Double entendres are another example of easily misunderstood statements. Here are some headlines that sound ridiculous (albeit hilarious) because of their double meanings:

- *Miners Refuse to Work After Death*
- *New Obesity Study Looks for Larger Test Group*
- *Children Make Nutritious Snacks*
- *Mechanic Finds Leak in Rear End*
- *Prostitutes Appeal to the Pope*
- *Stolen Painting Found by Tree*
- *Milk Drinkers are Turning to Powder*
- *Juvenile Court to Try Shooting Defendant*

- *Complaints bout NBA Referees Growing Ugly*
- *Panda Mating Fails, Veterinarian Takes Over*
- *Police Begin Campaign to Run Down Jaywalkers*
- *Two Sisters Reunited After Eighteen Years at Checkout Counter*
- *Man Eating Piranha Mistakenly Sold as Pet Fish*
- *Hospitals Sued by Seven Foot Doctors*
- *Two Soviet Ships Collide, One Dies*

While some of this can be chalked up to bad grammar, we have to remember that when being efficient and knowing what *we* want to communicate, our phrasing doesn't always come out as we want it to or isn't always understood in the same way we understand it. Restructuring what we want to say or taking time for clearer language can save us headaches, stress, from making moves in the wrong directions, and spreading faulty information that makes us have to unlearn what we have learned. Here's a few more phrases with multiple meanings:

Pass out—to distribute something OR to lose consciousness

Bring up—raise a child OR reference something

Take out—go on a date with OR kill OR pick up food to go

Back up—move backwards OR make an extra copy

Work out—exercise OR resolve

Make up—invent a story OR restore a relationship OR apply cosmetics

Bark—tree coating OR a dog's sound

Date—a type of fruit OR a romantic event

Dough—money OR bread

Even "We need to step up our game this quarter" can have unintended consequences without Clarity. I know I have said this and many other unclear phrases that I know exactly what it means, but my team doesn't. *"What 'game'? How far do we need to 'step up'? I didn't even know things were not where they should be."* These are the thoughts from my team when I come out with unclear messages and don't give them the clarity that they need and expect.

And don't get me started on emojis. I was communicating with a Polish person for work, and I put a thumbs-up emoji in my email rather than saying, "I agree with your comment." They replied that they did not understand what it was, and I could tell they were a little stressed in trying to figure it out. "Does this thumb mean Alex is upset, happy, or is it a mistake?" Were things good or bad?

As you can see, even in the everyday words and symbols we use, there is plenty of room for miscommunication. If we don't stop to think about how the other person might interpret what we are saying—let alone what information they may or may not already possess—we leave plenty of room for CAREless mistakes to occur.

Overcoming the Bias

So, what can we do to create better Clarity in our communication with our teams?

First and foremost, slow down before charging ahead with any communication. *Assume you are making assumptions*, and then dig in and explore what those assumptions might be. Bring in others with different perspectives and backgrounds. After meetings, or whenever communication has occurred, check to see that everyone is on the same page. Then double-check. Be humble and unafraid to ask questions. That is the best way to ensure you're all on the same page. Questions close the information gap and combat the Curse of Knowledge.

Here are a few questions to ask yourself before communicating with your team:

1. **Who am I talking to?** Knowing who you are discussing the topic or situation with will help you direct your energy, tone, and information. Their level of understanding should be taken into consideration as well as education and familiarity. How they absorb information will also help direct you in a way to present information effectively the first time.

2. **How can I test my assumptions of what they know versus what I know?** Establishing a way to test your presentations or practice them will not only bring more clarity the first time

around but build confidence too. You can film yourself and take notes on what you do. Reflecting on previous conversations and where people may have had, more or less, confusion will also be a good guide to testing your assumptions. Recall your earlier days in this position too, and think of what questions you had when you were in their shoes. Try to answer those. This also helps with building self-awareness and humility, as we talked about earlier.

3. **What gaps of knowledge may need to be filled in?** When you're using industry-specific jargon, it's best to spell it out beforehand and make sure you establish the full term before jumping to the acronym. Be ready to flip back to the full term if the acronym is causing confusion.

4. **What can I do to put people at ease and remove threats to psychological safety?** Consider your environment you're presenting in, the time of day, if it's in-person or online. Create space for people to ask questions during the presentation instead of just at the end. And preface your time that you are open to ideas, suggestions, feedback, or stopping to re-explain items before going further.

5. **How do I ensure they have a chance to communicate back what I have told them?** What mechanisms are in place? If you don't see a place to ask questions in your meeting or day-to-day working environment, establish them in a way that works best for you and your team. Ask them questions too, to get them thinking and spur conversations.

In addition to asking questions throughout the process, always assume less and clarify more. Reread all emails and written communications through the eyes of the recipient. Be as clear, concise, and simple as possible. Sometimes it helps to give emails a waiting period before you send them. You'll see the ambiguities and assumptions in them and be able to revise so there is a higher chance for Clarity the first time around.

Finally, be humble and transparent. You don't need to have all the answers. Stop trying to be a hero or the smartest person in the room.

It's okay not to know. Instead of having a CAREless attitude, such as, *"Why aren't they listening to me?"* have a CAREful attitude: *"How can I better provide the details they need to do better?"*

> It's okay not to know.

Stop assuming, start asking. Clarify more, assume less. Knowing means not assuming. Get on the same page before you start anything. Put people's brains at cognitive ease by being clear and concise. Build psychological safety so people feel comfortable asking questions. Silence is good for no one.

Let's Work It

Here's an exercise you can try, to illustrate some of the issues with the Curse of Knowledge. You'll need to borrow a coworker, a friend, or a partner. Choose one of the images below, and without showing the other person the picture or hinting in any way at what it depicts, give them written or verbal instructions on how to draw the image.

When your friend is finished, compare their drawing to the image(s) above. How close did they get? Were they able to follow your instructions? How many bad assumptions did you make? How many did they make? How many miscues occurred? Did you find yourself frustrated at all? Was your partner frustrated because they didn't have enough Clarity? How could you have explained things more clearly?

START-STOP-CONTINUE EXERCISE

Ask yourself these start-stop-continue questions:

Start—*What am not currently doing that I should* start *doing to help me reduce the Curse of Knowledge?*

Stop—*What am I doing now that I should* stop *doing that is causing the Curse of Knowledge?*

Continue—*What is working for me that I should* continue *doing?*

Simply being aware of biases, such as the Curse of Knowledge, can improve the way you communicate and collaborate with other humans. In the next chapter, you'll learn how another Clarity bias will help you positively influence others. It is a bias that politicians and advertisers often use to their advantage.

CHAPTER 5

CLARITY BIAS #2
THE FRAMING EFFECT

The Framing Effect is a cognitive bias whereby people react differently to the same information when it is communicated in different ways. Our decisions and judgments can be influenced more by the *way* information is framed than by the information itself. For example, we often react differently to information based on whether it is presented as a gain or a loss.

Here's a scenario: you are asked to bet $100, and the odds that you will either double your bet or lose it all are 50/50.

Version A: "You have a 50 percent chance of winning $100!"

Version B: "You have a 50 percent chance of losing your $100."

Although the expected outcome of both options is the same, people tend to prefer Version A, which presents the situation as a potential gain, to Version B, which presents it as a potential loss. People are more likely to bet their money when presented with Version A. Ergo, framing affects our actions. It's important to start with the facts and then think carefully about how to effectively frame those facts for the receiver.

The Framing Effect

Sometimes I get feedback from my team that if I had presented a topic differently, it would have been better received. Here is a real Alexample of communication I said over the phone, believe it or not:

> "You have four weeks to save your job," I said and then proceeded to outline the things this person needed to work on. Imagine being on the receiving end of that sentence. Would you have taken in anything that came after such an opener? Here is what I should have said: "Let's create a four-week plan to get you to a place that is within the clear expectations of someone in your role."

The bias: The *way* information is communicated affects the way we think about that information and act upon it—often more than the information itself.

The effect on Clarity: When we say one thing with our actual words but communicate something different in the way we frame those words, Clarity can be muddied, and performance can be affected.

The cure: *Stop* unintentionally framing ideas in a way that works against your team's best performance. *Start* being conscious of the way you frame ideas.

Frames Over Facts

A *mental frame* is a cognitive structure that organizes information in the brain. Frames help people make sense of the world by providing context for interpreting and categorizing new information. When we're the ones doing the communicating, we often frame our ideas in a deliberately chosen way so as to influence other people's thoughts and behaviors. Sometimes, however, we do this framing unconsciously, as shaped by our experiences, whether parenting, schooling, beliefs, values, cultural background, or something else. Similarly, when we're the *recipients* of communication, sometimes we are aware of the framing used; other times it affects us unconsciously.

Mental frames influence how we perceive, interpret, and remember information. We can only understand what the frames in our brains allow us to understand. They help us filter information and focus on what is relevant and important, to decipher what is "good" over "bad." Frames also influence our decision-making by shaping how we evaluate options and weigh trade-offs and by how we make goals for the future.

For example, a person who holds a mental frame (consciously or unconsciously) that "money buys happiness" will be more likely to prioritize financial gain over other goals, while someone who holds a mental frame that "nothing matters more than your health" will usually prioritize health over financial gain when making decisions.

Frames can be more even powerful than facts, as today's political rhetoric graphically demonstrates. In cases where the facts don't fit the frames, the frames often prevail, and the facts are ignored.

Frames tend to dwell in our cognitive unconscious—a place we have difficulty accessing. However, with increased self-awareness, we can become more conscious of the frames we carry around and employ. Understanding the mental frames that shape our thinking will help us become more aware of our biases and make more informed decisions.

Framing in the Workplace

From a leadership perspective, the Framing Effect simply means that the words you choose and the attitudes you project, whether in person or written out, have a powerful influence on how people interpret the information you are presenting.

As illustrated earlier, if a choice is presented in a "gain" framework, emphasizing the potential benefits rather than the disadvantages, people are more likely to choose that option. A simple positive frame, rather than a negative one, can make an action more palatable. For example, instead of telling a team member, "Sorry, but I have some grunt work for you," you might say instead, "I have a task for you that is really valuable to us because it supports us in *XYZ* ways and will help us accomplish [goal *x*]." The same task is presented in both cases, but the mode of framing will likely elicit a different level of engagement.

However, people also tend to be powerfully loss-averse, so in some cases, they are more likely to take action when it is framed in terms of *avoiding a loss* rather than courting an opportunity. "If you don't take [Step A] by March 15, you risk a serious fine" is more likely to spur action than "Take [Step B] by March 15 in order to qualify for our special bonus!" It's up to you to know and adapt to who you are communicating to and what task is at hand so you know how to frame this effectively for the person on the receiving end.

The Framing Effect is used by communicators in all kinds of scenarios, from marketing and healthcare decisions to politics. Politicians strive to find ways to wrap their platforms in positive packaging, such as "Pro-Life," "Build Back Better," "Make America Great Again," or "American Rescue." They do this to make it easy for people to side with their initiatives and hard for people to oppose them. After all, who wants to be seen as anti-life? Who supports making America lousy or building back worse? *You'd have to be evil or an idiot to oppose this platform!* is the underlying message of such framing.

If you want to have Clarity in your communications, it is vital that you become conscious of the Framing Effect. When your framing is congruent with the message you are trying to send, Clarity shines; everybody understands the message and knows what to do. However, when the framing is at odds with the message you purport to send, Clarity falters. People don't know what to do and their threat circuitry is triggered.

Remember, people ultimately pay more attention to the framing than the words.

"Corporate" wants us to do it

Here is an example from the business world. The C-suite of a company has committed to a set of diversity, equity, and inclusion initiatives as part of a cultural revamp. Some of the changes include discussion groups, compliance trainings, and new incentive programs. Implementing these changes will take a lot of buy-in from people at every level of the company. The senior executives explain the new measures to the mid-level managers so that they can, in turn, communicate the message to their frontline teams. But some of the managers don't really believe there are any diversity or inclusion issues within *their* departments. They see the trainings as a way to win over the younger managers. In other words, a well-intentioned waste of time.

So one of the managers, when presenting the new initiatives to their direct reports, frames it this way: "Corporate wants you all to complete some new compliance training on diversity. There are also some optional groups you can join up with. You can talk to HR for more info." They throw in an ever-so-subtle eye roll at the end.

The manager's framing drastically altered the meaning and strength of the original message. What the team members heard was: "Corporate is making us do these compliance trainings that our manager doesn't believe in. We can probably get away with giving it minimal effort."

What the manager could have said, using an energetic voice and encouraging body language, was, "I need you all to complete these trainings with full commitment and enthusiasm. It'll be important for organizational alignment in the long run." Clarity would have thus prevailed. The team members would have received the undiluted, congruently delivered message: "These trainings are important, so we should take them seriously."

"Wipe out bad leadership" or . . .

This example just so happens to be mine. DX's purpose is to wipe out bad leadership. We market this to HR folks in organizations. If the mental frame through which they typically see their world is, "Our leaders here are awesome," then no matter how many facts we send them about how their leadership is failing in the twenty-first century, their reaction will be to ignore us or challenge us. They may even feel threatened by our message.

If, on the other hand, our "wipe out bad leadership" message is received by someone who is having a hard time filling roles at their company because of well-publicized leadership issues, it will probably be received with open arms and an offer to buy us a few drinks.

So, is our marketing better served by saying, "We develop great leaders," or, "We wipe out bad leadership"? Depends on whom we're talking to. If *our* framing is at odds with *their* inner framing, our message won't be received. Clarity will fizzle out before it has a chance to flourish. When you communicate with the preferences and attitudes of those you serve in mind, you increase the chances that the idea you're presenting will be met with receptivity. Your framing lines up with theirs, and your message can get through on a clear signal.

Common Types of Framing

Framing occurs in different ways. Probably the most pervasive way is simply through our voice and body—the way we speak our messages.

Expressional framing

The tone in which we say something as well as our facial expressions and body language can heavily impact the way others interpret its meaning. Our vocal quality, posture, and physical gestures communicate volumes about whether we believe in the message we're speaking or not. Do we appear apologetic? Bored? Annoyed? When we want our team—or anyone—to embrace a new idea, it is vital that we present it with bright facial expressions, energized voices, and appropriate body language. People glean far more meaning from our expressional mode of delivery than from the words themselves.

Take the simple words, "You suck." When we say them with a twinkle in our eye, the recipient knows we're kidding, but when we say them with a clenched jaw, they cut deep.

Albert Mehrabian, a noted psychologist and body language researcher, performed research on communication and discovered that in situations where verbal and nonverbal meanings were incongruous with one another:

- Only 7 percent of the message's impact came from the words themselves (verbal content);
- 38 percent of the message's impact came from paralinguistic cues (tone of voice, pitch, etc.); and
- 55 percent of the message's impact came from nonverbal cues (facial expressions, gestures, body language, etc.).

Mehrabian's findings have been misinterpreted a bit in popular literature, but what we should take from his research is that both verbal and nonverbal forms of communication are vitally important. And, in some cases, the nonverbal might be more important, especially when clarity is lacking in communication.

Most of us are not fully aware of the way we present ourselves and the effect we have on others. That's why when you are in a leadership position, it can be helpful to receive coaching on your presentational skills or record yourself, study what you're doing, and make adjustments. It has often been pointed out that in the first televised presidential debates—Nixon vs. Kennedy in 1962—Nixon likely lost the election because of his habit of repeatedly shifting his eyes. People thought he looked dishonest. His words no longer mattered. Many have speculated that if the debate had been broadcast on radio only, Nixon would have won.

When your expressional delivery is incongruent with the words you are speaking, Clarity suffers. People get a mixed message instead of a clear one. For example, if you say, "I have some exciting news" with slumped shoulders and the vocal enthusiasm of an anemic barnacle, your audience won't know whether to believe you. When you say, "I'm listening," but you fold your arms and frown, people read defensiveness. I have seen leaders literally shaking their heads no while saying, "I agree," and smiling when they announce layoffs. Clarity? Not so much.

In addition to practicing your presentational skills, the key to creating more congruence in your messaging is to align yourself internally. Before sharing a message with others, make sure you are fully onboard yourself. If you are, your belief in what you are saying will shine through naturally. If you are not, people will sense your disconnect.

Audio-visual framing

Framing occurs in written communications as well. The style and form in which you present your message must fully align with the message itself in order for Clarity to prevail. If you want someone to hire you as an editor, for example, don't send out a cover letter filled with typos and poor grammar. If you are creating upscale marketing material about quality workmanship, don't use cheesy clip art and Microsoft Word fonts.

As poets and advertisers know, word *choice* matters. Words have both *de*notations (explicit meanings) and *con*notations (implicit meanings). For instance, the word *fangirl* denotes essentially the same concept as *connoisseur* but carries a vastly different set of connotations. Choose your words carefully. Get a second opinion before sending anything out.

Auditory and visual components are vital aspects of framing when presenting information in video format. Movie directors are well aware of the power that music and sound effects have on the way the audience interprets a scene. There are numerous YouTube videos that demonstrate this, and most are hilarious. There's one that takes a notoriously suspenseful sequence from *Breaking Bad* and sets it to goofy sitcom music and a laugh track. The effect of the scene is entirely transformed. Make sure you're not framing your message with words or audio in ways that contradict or undermine it.

Value framing

Value framing can mean a couple of different things. It can refer to using psychological techniques to alter the perceived value of an offered choice (i.e., make us feel we're getting a better deal than we might otherwise perceive). Emailed sales letters make flagrant use of this type of value framing.

From a leadership perspective, value framing can also refer to the use of human values as a way to create buy-in for an idea. Insurance companies, for example, tap into our desire to care responsibly for our families as a way to sell us life insurance policies. Pharmaceutical companies sell us on the value of living long, happy lives—their ads depict smiling elders riding on horses and playing with their grandchildren—to entice us to buy their medications. Politicians cloak their ideas in religious values to get our vote.

As leaders, we employ value framing when using our company's mission as a way to motivate and inspire team members or when we use the values of financial stability and career prestige as ways to retain employees for the long term. Value framing can be a subtle or not-so-subtle way to nudge our people toward making the choice *we* want them to make: "Are we going to build for the future or stay mired in the past?"

Value framing is powerful, but you must use it consciously and scrupulously. Clarity can suffer if you use conflicting values in your framing, such as "Have fun" and "Buckle down." If people feel they have been manipulated, misled, or deceived, this can quickly erode any psychological safety you have built and any client trust as well.

Positive vs. negative framing

There has been a longstanding debate as to whether positive or negative framing works better. Positive framing (such as "This product is 80 percent fat-free") often works much better than the negative framing ("This product contains 20 percent fat"). We all prefer to focus on the upsides of a choice, not the downsides.

On the other hand, plenty of studies suggest that "negative" framing has a powerful and motivating effect on us as well. Fear of loss, for example, is routinely used as a sales motivator. Marketers often use this ploy to prompt us to take action quickly. "Last chance to save!" or "This great offer ends at midnight tonight!" The intention of this frame is to make people feel they will lose something if they don't act. As noted earlier, people tend to take action to avoid painful losses more readily than to gain positive benefits. Fear of dying can be a much stronger motivator of behavior changes—such as quitting smoking or losing weight—than "I want to have good health."

In business, sometimes negative framing is necessary and helpful. If a company's survival is threatened, you may need to share this information with employees and use it to frame their options. Fear of losing their income and valued work relationships can spur them to come up with innovative ideas or increase their productivity. In a hiring situation, a company might be on the fence about taking you on board. Framing your "Thanks for the interview" letter with a mention that you have a job offer from another company can push them over the fence. (Don't lie about a job offer if you don't have one, but if it's true, don't be afraid to mention it!) Providing Clarity about your situation will frame their reaction to be more in line with what you want, and the fear of losing you to another employer might spur them into making an offer.

I used this to get my wife to date me. I met her online. She ignored the first email I sent, but I had a feeling in my gut that I shouldn't give up. So, I persisted, sending several more emails. Nothing. Not wishing to appear stalker-y, I wrote a final email saying something along the lines of, "This is my last email. I will be switching this profile off, so if you are interested in meeting up for lunch, this is your last chance." She reached out. She'd been intrigued by me initially it turned out, but not enough to overcome her resistance to dating yet another guy who was probably pursuing her only for her looks. Taking myself "off the market" provoked just enough sense of potential loss that she agreed to meet me. We are now happily married with two children.

Which framing works better? Here are some ways various groups reacted to both:

- 93 percent of PhD students registered early when a penalty fee for late registration was emphasized, with only 67 percent doing so when the price change was presented as a discount for earlier registration (negative framing wins).[1]

- More people will support an economic policy when the employment rate is emphasized than when the associated unemployment rate is highlighted (positive framing wins).[2]
- The Advertising Research Council reported that televised messages encouraging men to consult their doctors about potential colon cancer resulted in a doubling of inquiries to physicians (negative framing wins).[3]
- It has been argued that pretrial detention increases a defendant's willingness to accept a plea bargain, since pleading guilty will be viewed as an event that will cause his earlier release rather than as an event that will put him in prison (positive framing wins).[4]

The bottom line is that both negative and positive framing can be effective. But you need to be consciously aware of the *type* you use and the purpose you are using it for. In a leadership context, it is my belief that positive framing is preferable most of the time. Doing a good job because you want to build a better future for yourself and your company is vastly more empowering over the long term than doing a good job because you're afraid of getting fired. The "I'll fire your ass if you don't produce" framing tends to create stress over time, and stress saps people's ability to think and contribute at their highest levels. It also creates an oppositional relationship between you and your team, rather than one where you are all rowing together toward the same destination.

The last thing you want to do is inadvertently create negative framing—whether it's your body language, tone of voice, or the way you "package" an idea—when positive framing is what you want. Or vice versa. That is when Clarity suffers. Your framing must be congruent with your message if you want Clarity to prevail.

Overcoming and Utilizing the Bias

Framing occurs whether we know it or not. But the Framing Effect is not only a bias; it is also a potential tool in our leadership toolbelt.

We need to get control of it so that our framing is fully in line with whatever message we are trying to send.

The idea is not so much to frame information so that people do what you want but rather to be conscious of the frames you use and how they can affect your team. It's about understanding the role context plays in communication. For example, if you say to your team, "I don't want you to be anchored by what our competitor is doing," you may be unintentionally influencing them to draw comparisons to your competitors. It's about understanding the power of nonverbal communication and how it can affect your team's actions. And yes, it's also about being a skillful leader who can effectively communicate initiatives.

How does all this relate to Clarity? When our framing is fully in line with our intentions, we deliver a clear and cohesive message. Conversely, when the receiver senses a disconnect between what we're saying and the *way* we're saying it, ambiguity and confusion arise. The cognitive stress triggers the threat circuitry, and your team will not speak up to ask questions, which always leads to problems down the road.

Understanding your use of the Framing Effect will keep you from misleading people and, potentially, taking them down a road they weren't expecting. There is a fine line between motivation and deception. As a leader, you are always supplying a lens through which your team views the goals and initiatives you present. When you intentionally or unintentionally change the meaning of the information being presented, you influence how the information is understood. Be aware of this at all times. Don't undersell, oversell, or mis-sell an idea with your framing. Using framing tools effectively and ethically is the key to their success. Our job as leaders is to positively influence those we serve, but we're not being positive if we lead them down a path they were not expecting.

Let's Work It

Culture is becoming more and more integral to how organizations attract, retain, and develop people. As the expectations of newer generations change from those of older generations, organizations need to adapt and evolve. Maybe they said they were a collaborative environment and wanted people to bring new ideas to the table, but there hasn't been an opportunity for you to express these. Or maybe they said they are respectful of a life-work balance with only rare exceptions for overtime, but you find that you are constantly pressured to take work home and work on weekends.

Can you think of a time when you felt misled by what the organization's website and hiring manager said about the culture of the organization you were about to join and the reality of what it was really like? What expectations did you have after seeing the job listing and speaking with the hiring manager? What was the reality of the job compared to its description? How were these expectations created? What role did the Framing Effect play in this? Was more than one form of framing type employed?

Think of a time when your team felt confused or misled by you. In what ways did you consciously employ the Framing Effect? Looking back, did you use some unconscious framing as well? How might have you used the Framing Effect differently to produce a different outcome?

START-STOP-CONTINUE EXERCISE

Ask yourself these start-stop-continue questions:

Start—*What am I not doing that I need to* start *doing, to use the Framing Effect more effectively?*

Stop—*What am I currently doing that I need to* stop *doing, to use the Framing Effect more effectively?*

Continue—*What am I currently doing that I should* continue *doing, that is using the Framing Effect effectively?*

ON CLARITY

Clarity is all about providing those you serve with a sense of certainty so that your team can be at cognitive ease and can produce in a relaxed, stress-free, psychologically safe environment. How do you get on top of these cognitive biases so that you can continue to create Clarity within your team or organization?

Don't jump in and let your brain get the better of you. Slow things down so you can check your biases and therefore your assumptions before opening your mouth. Slow is smooth; smooth is fast. When we find time in our busy schedules to slow down and reflect, ask questions, get curious, and challenge the assumptions our brain is making so we can gain crystal-clear clarity with ourselves and those we serve, we will actually go faster. There is less rework, duplication of efforts, random phone calls asking for more information, and less stress when clarity is provided the first time around. By doing the opposite of what the brain wants—run fast and make assumptions—in the beginning, your work will be smoother, your team will be more efficient during the process, and you'll end up working faster. Slow is smooth. And smooth is fast. Something as simple as asking if they meant Canadian or US dollars can save time, money, and resources versus the alternative: walking away not knowing what was actually meant, not saying anything about it, and having to waste time and energy figuring it out for yourself.

You know your team does *not* feel safe when everyone remains quiet and they all keep to themselves to avoid looking stupid. Silence kills leadership. Silence kills high-performing teams.

You know your team feels "safe" when they ask you for more Clarity. They freely come to you with requests for more information because they want to ensure crystal-clear alignment with you and their teammates. They're able to do this because their threat circuitry is not triggered. They don't see you as a saber-toothed tiger. You have not cursed them with your amazing knowledge, and you have not tried to manipulate them through sneaky frames. Rather, you have simply let them know (1) what is expected of them, (2) why it is expected of them, (3) when they're expected to do what they need to do, and (4) whom they can go to for help. As Brené Brown states, "To be clear is to be kind."

CLARITY is the WHAT.

The clearer the "What," the better things are for those we serve, and the further on your way you are to having Clarity lead to psychological safety for your team.

Now we're ready to look at the "How." Let's get into Autonomy, the next pillar of CARE.

PART II

Clarity

Autonomy

Relationships

Equity

CHAPTER 6

THE IMPORTANCE OF
AUTONOMY

"I *love* being told how to do my job!" said no one ever. Equally popular is the experience of being micromanaged. Overmanagement puts shackles on our creativity and capability.

To be given Autonomy is to be given freedom. And trust. It is to be told, "We value your skills and knowledge, and we want you to apply them as you see fit as you perform your role." Autonomy means that when you are acting in your role with the Clarity given to you, you know people trust you and your expertise to do what is best for the task at hand and that your method of work is effective enough to achieve the results expected of you.

To provide Autonomy, a leader must acknowledge that what works best for them may not work for others, and they must trust that their team members know their own best approach, their own "How" to "get sh*t done." If you are hiring for talent, don't stifle them by forcing them to work your way. Hire talented people, give them clear direction, and get out of *their* way. So long as your people have a clear idea of "Why" they are doing this, "What" they are needing to be doing, "When" it's due, and "Who" is working on the project, "How" they get that done should be left up to them. That's why you hired them—you trust them to get it done. The clearer your Clarity is that provides them all the other information, the more autonomy should be given and vice versa.

Defining Autonomy

Remember the famous scene in *Braveheart* when William Wallace with his face painted blue rides in on his horse to rally an army of angry Scotsman against the tyrannical English king, Edward the First? "They may take our lives, but they will never take our FREEDOM!" he screams, as the men stand behind him, swords raised, shouting in unison, *"Alba gu bràth!"* (Scotland forever!)

Maybe you've been tempted to march into your manager's office adorned in blue face paint and a kilt to demand a little independence, trust, or respect. Or maybe your team members have been tempted to do the same to you.

This "freedom" and independence we all crave leads us to the next part of the CARE Equation: *Autonomy*. Whereas Clarity is easy to identify (either you're crystal clear on things or you're not), Autonomy is more of a graded perception or *feeling*, and the need for Autonomy varies from person to person and situation to situation. So, how do you create the feeling—in yourself and those you lead—of *"I have enough Autonomy based on the situation"*?

Before you assume the way to Autonomy is running around in a kilt yelling, "FREEDOM!" like Mel Gibson, define what Autonomy means to you. I've heard many people say that it means they are entrusted, empowered, in control, or able to make decisions on their own. Whatever your definition is of Autonomy, write it down. After doing that, try infusing your working definition of Autonomy with some of these ideas:

- the ability to think for yourself
- the feeling that you have a genuine say in decision-making and a measure of control in at least your piece of the puzzle
- flexibility and knowing there are many ways to get from A to B
- the freedom to learn new skills for accomplishing your goals
- solving problems your way

My definition of Autonomy, from a leadership perspective, is *trusting your team to do what needs to be done, on their terms.*

Remember when you learned to drive a car and the feeling that came over you when you finally had that license in your hand? You suddenly had the freedom to hit the open road, stereo blasting, no instructor or parent grasping the door handle in terror. You still had (and currently have) rules to follow, but as long as you played the game correctly, you could drive that car wherever you wanted.

Don't you want those you lead to have that same feeling?

Of course, it's important to remember the journey required to get a license. When you sat behind the wheel for the first time, did the instructor say, "Okay, let 'er rip—you're in the driver's seat!" No. Your instructor gave you a specific set of instructions before even letting you put the key into the ignition, then you drove around an empty lot for a long time. Giving you full control of the car when you were a newbie would have been dangerous for everyone involved. And it

> Autonomy is not just handed out; it's earned . . .

would have felt overwhelming to you—perhaps scaring you from driving forever.

Autonomy is not just handed out; it's earned through wisdom and confidence. The more wisdom and confidence you acquire over time, the more control you want and deserve, so the more you should be given. Think about driving again. As you gain more wisdom and confidence at the wheel, you naturally crave more control, and the instructor gives you more opportunities to *take* control, even at the risk of making a few mistakes.

Autonomy and Clarity Go Hand in Hand

The ability to fail and learn is like being given a box to play in. The edges of the box are the boundaries—the clarity given by the leader. The leader provides the clarity by making sure there are answers to the questions: "Why are we doing this?", "What exactly needs to get done? When by?", and "Who needs to be involved?" The team member(s) can then choose the "How"—how things are executed, handled, stopped, started—through their Autonomy. But Clarity *must* come before Autonomy.

Questions can help shape the size and dimensions of the box, such as:

- Why are we doing this?
- What are the goals and expectations?
- When do we need to do it?
- Who else needs to be involved?

The answers to these and other questions provides Clarity to the person you are leading. Within the box, the team member then feels more confident, so they are free to "play" and solve problems in their own way.

Remember, not all boxes are equal. The person and the situation will determine the size of the box—the amount of Autonomy given to a team member. Some situations demand tighter control and less autonomy, but as leaders, we should always provide the fullest amount of autonomy practically possible. Everyone craves Autonomy to some extent, no matter what role they're serving, but some require more than others. *Give people the size box that suits their needs.*

What happens if you give people a box without any Clarity? Worse, if key questions go unanswered? Chaos and confusion.

Autonomy without Clarity = chaos and confusion

Clarity without Autonomy = micromanagement

No Clarity and no Autonomy = leaderless

Clarity and Autonomy = high-performance zone

Clarity and Autonomy are joined at the hip and require a continual balancing act. One does not work without the other. If your team knows what's expected of them, then, by building upon this foundation of Clarity, you can trust and empower them to meet those expectations with Autonomy—unless and until they show you otherwise.

For a leader to give people control, their team must have crystal-clear expectations, a mutual understanding of what needs to be done, and alignment toward a collective goal. When those conditions are met, control *must* be given. If a leader is telling everyone how to do things and not allowing people to figure things out on their own, who is in control? The leader is. Not the team member.

Trust your Team, Win in Business

The big emphasis with Autonomy is trust, and this is a huge part of building psychological safety within your team and winning. By giving team members a box to play in—and the freedom to play in it—you say to them, "You are trusted." You also say, "I value your knowledge and experience, and I want you to use it as you see fit."

Your team needs that sense that they are free to drive the car with no one looking over their shoulder. To continue to "sit in the front seat with them" is to rob them of trust.

At the start of the pandemic, my neighbor told me that when she was sent home to work remotely, her boss would demand proof of the work she was doing every literal minute of the day. There was *zero* trust (low Autonomy). Imagine the work that could have been accomplished in the hour she spent every day documenting her activities and actions.

Don't be that boss. You'll have no one left to lead by the end of it. The temptation as a leader in a hybrid (or remote) workplace is to want to see people's work being done in even more detail than when they were in the office. But the opposite is what you should aim for: remote workers must be given an increased level of Autonomy; otherwise, you will spend your entire time micromanaging their workflow.

When people started working from home in the pandemic, companies were forced to trust that work would still get done. And it was! But when team members all across the board were forced to come back into the office under the guise of "productivity will increase," those who succeeded in a remote-working environment felt their leaders didn't trust them and that they had no Autonomy over their working environment. Their preferences for working when and where they wanted to do better didn't matter to their leader; the leader wanted it done *their way*, even if it meant less work was getting done. But companies that have empowered their employees by giving them more Autonomy (picking where they work, when they work, and how they get that work done) are seeing improvements in nearly every aspect of the employee experience, from productivity to motivation and engagement, and ultimately to the bottom line.

Autonomy is also closely connected to *latitude*, the knowledge that they can bring in their own thoughts and ideas to the table. Dr. Rick Nauert reported that *"When people feel that they have latitude, the results are greater employee commitment, better performance, improved productivity and lower turnover."*[1] In other words, it's not a my-way-or-the-highway environment but one that lets a team member know that their boss gives them the latitude (freedom/Autonomy) to do whatever it is in the best way possible. It enables them to do their best work.

When that trust and latitude are given, their response is often: "Of course I will be more committed and perform better. I am allowed to do what you hired me to do so I will produce more and am less likely to listen to the ever-growing number of recruiter calls and LinkedIn messages I get every day." Latitude goes a long way.

When you steal people's Autonomy, you are stealing the treasured ability to grow and develop. How we want to grow and develop is different for everyone, but when it's taken away, they feel like they can't do anything good enough for you. What happens then? You lose trust and unity within your team. Innovative ideas dwindle. Performance falls off. Engagement levels drop. People start looking for opportunities elsewhere, places where their talents are appreciated and where they are given a chance to grow and develop better.

We all crave being in control. *Why?* In the old days if it was cold, we would build a fire. If there was a dinosaur attack, we'd run to our cave. If we cut ourselves badly, we'd tie cloth around the wound. We as humans are more comfortable when *we* are in control of our environment. When someone else tries to control us, it triggers the threat circuitry. Don't unnecessarily steal control of those you serve. A CAREing leader provides Autonomy so every person on their team can feel they are positioned to succeed. That is how effective leaders CARE, and that's how they CARE to Win.

Alexample in Autonomy

I will never forget the day I stole my team's Autonomy.

DX Learning had reached a decision point regarding two technology vendors for a client project. We had worked with one for some time, and I had a good relationship with their CEO. I regarded him as a friend and partner—still do—and our visions for a more human world were aligned. However, his company was early on in its journey in developing the technology we needed. In our first forays of piloting their software, we had issues that were dragging down both his team and ours. We mutually agreed that I should check out another vendor.

We found an alternative, and my team had all done its research. The moment of truth had arrived. Due to a looming client deadline, we needed to make a decision during a Monday morning meeting. Which vendor would we choose: the old one or the new one? I had spent the weekend prior debating with myself and had changed my choice a number of times. But I woke up on Monday, clear as day as to how we should proceed. I started the meeting with, "I've made a decision. We're going with the existing vendor."

Insert slide trombone sound. The looks of dismay and horror around the table told me I had made a mistake, and the onslaught began. I'm lucky I have a great team that feels psychologically safe enough to call me out when I'm wrong. This was one of those times.

I shut my mouth. I listened and learned and changed my mind based on their input. I was wrong; they were right. We've not looked back since.

But what if they hadn't felt psychologically safe enough to disagree? What if they simply complied with my decision and then disengaged later on? I know I would be out at least one team member right now. I should have approached the meeting differently. Perhaps I could have started instead with, "My intention is to make a decision on vendors today; let's hear your thoughts on both of them." How do you think that would have played out?

Starting sentences with "My intention . . ." as opposed to, say, "I've made a decision . . ." is a great idea from the book *Turn This Ship Around* by David Marquet. He reversed the performance of the lowest-performing sub in the American Navy by adopting an inclusive and empowering mindset. By starting sentences with "My intention . . ." you imply you're open to change. You invite input. You engage your team in the process and give them a voice. You then honor that voice when it comes to the distribution of roles and the execution of tasks.

I'm not always right. Nor are you. Your team is not always right either, but you must trust *their* intentions and approach each conversation with a flexible mindset. You must seek their opinions and be open to change based on what you hear. Leverage their collective IQ and experience by empowering them to speak up. This is where the importance of psychological safety comes in. A leader creates a safe place where everyone has a voice and everyone feels their input is valued. That's where ideas and creativity are born, leading to higher performance.

By contrast, nothing is more anti-Autonomy than the statement, "This is how we've always done it." That is the all-in-one killer of innovation, engagement, and performance. There was a time the team asked me what we should do as a holiday thank-you for our clients. My reply: "We always just send a card signed by all of us." So, we did the same old same old. The following year I asked the team the same question. Their idea blew my mind: customized DX cookies, homemade right in Chicago, with some of the proceeds going to a local charity. Our clients loved it. It embodied one of our core values, being customer centric, way more than a stodgy old card.

Give Autonomy, Get Back Productivity and Creativity

We have a saying at DX Learning: "The person who does the talking does the learning." Think about it. When you're talking, your brain is synthesizing information much faster—and much more creatively—than when you're listening. Maybe that's why teachers, doctors, coaches, CEOs, and professors seem to know so much. Because they keep on talking. We were given two ears and one mouth; we should use them in that ratio.

> The person who does the talking does the learning.

The teacher often learns more than the student—especially when teaching a new subject or teaching in a new way. It might sound counterintuitive, but if I'm talking, my brain is striving to think of solutions and to connect the dots to my own experiences. It is actively building fresh connections between ideas in ways it doesn't have to do when processing information passively (listening). It is working to develop a cohesive train of thought. As the speaker, I am in control of the learning event. When I am listening, I am not in control. I am in a receptive role.

When a leader tells their employees how to do things, *they're* in control. The team member who is not in control will eventually see this as a threat. Why? Well, several reasons. We all know that no one looks out for our interests the way we do. We trust our firsthand knowledge and experience more than we trust anything else. When someone else takes unnecessary control of our tasks, the implication is that we can't decide for ourselves how best to accomplish our work; that we don't have the knowledge, skills, or ability to do our job effectively; and that we weren't really hired for our specialized talents and insights but rather to just do as we're told. And that means we must either compromise our self-actualization to stay in this job or seek fulfillment elsewhere.

According to Harvard University's School of Public Health, "A lack of control over important aspects of one's work life is highly stressful"—to the point of causing serious health problems.[2] Again we see how, under stress, the brain reduces the resources flowing to those areas where higher thinking takes place and reallocates them to primary survival functions. Thus, having little Autonomy compromises higher thinking. And how can you be at your best if you're not thinking clearly or making good decisions?

Implications for leaders

One way to jumpstart Autonomy is by getting people to talk. As a leader, when you ask team members questions such as, "If this was your decision, how would you do it?" or "What are some options available to us?" and listen to their answers, you pass Autonomy to them. Because now *they* are the ones doing the talking, which makes them feel in control. When *you're* doing the talking, *you* are the one in control.

Don't let your team fall into the habit of complying with your control and thus disengaging. They go silent, and what does that do to a team? Silence kills business. Silence kills leadership. Silence kills relationships.

Get them talking every day and especially every time a solution is needed. When people talk, they are taking ownership, connecting ideas in new ways, thinking, "Oh, here's a way to do it." This excites and engages their brain. It believes it's in control and does not go into the partial shutdown caused by stress. Now everyone wins. You have a team member who is actively engaged, and you reap the benefits of their creative problem-solving.

Curiosity beats advice

In *The Advice Trap*, Michael Bungay Stanier's brilliant sequel to *The Coaching Habit*, Stanier talks about shifting from leading by advice to leading by curiosity. He says, "Turns out curiosity is a superpower: it increases engagement and impact. But its kryptonite is the Advice Monster."[3] If you are talking more than you are listening—always jumping in to offer ideas, opinions, suggestions—you aren't effectively leading. Our job as leaders is to ask questions and create inquisitiveness via curiosity. *Ask more, tell less.*

Every time you answer a question or jump in to solve a problem, you are not only sacrificing your own productive time, but you are also failing to empower your team members to think for themselves, which ends up stealing their Autonomy. Every time you micromanage or do a job yourself, you steal control from others, *and* you rob you of your own effectiveness. Your head is now down, doing the work, and you're no longer seeing what's going on around you. On the other hand, when you resist your brain's desire for control and let others think and do the work, your head is up, and you can see the big picture. You have more time to do higher-level things.

Lead with questions, lead with empowerment, and seize back time you can use for focusing on high-level tasks and building Relationships—the next important piece of the CARE equation—with your team and your clients.

Psychological Safety and Autonomy

Before we look at some of the biases that can prevent us from creating Autonomy within our teams, let's talk a little more about psychological safety. In her book, *The Fearless Organization*, which I referred to earlier, Amy Edmondson suggests there are three pieces to creating psychological safety.[4] They are:

1. Set the stage for your people.
2. Invite input.
3. Always respond productively.

To set the stage (1) means to be clear about what you're doing, why you're doing it, and what your expectations are. This goes back to our first piece of the CARE equation, Clarity.

Inviting input (2) is the next step and a great start to creating Autonomy. Always lead with, "I don't have all the answers to this, and I need your help," or "My intentions are . . ." Create a space for everyone—not just the loudest a**hole in the room—to have a voice. This is a crucial aspect of psychological safety.

When your team does contribute, always respond productively (3), and thank them for their input. Never get angry, cut them off, ignore them, or interrupt them, and don't let your emotions get the best of you. If you do, they may never speak up again.

You also need to say what's on *your* mind. Share your imperfect ideas. Be vulnerable and open to criticism. This will model for your team how to do the same thing. Imagine having to go home every night carrying the emotional baggage of all the things you wished you said but didn't because a little voice was saying, "Don't speak up." The power of psychological safety shines when no one, including you, has to go home and worry about what they *could* have said. Why? Because they said it.

A lack of psychological safety can lead to the illusion of success. Leaders who welcome only good news ultimately create fear of failure in their companies. They find themselves surrounded by "yes-people" who are afraid to tell the emperor he is buck naked.

> A lack of psychological safety can lead to the illusion of success.

Vulnerability Is a Strength

No one—leader or team member—wants to look stupid or ignorant. The brain wants to be right. It hates being wrong and it doesn't like to be challenged. It wants you to appear capable, knowledgeable, and helpful in the eyes of others.

We fear that asking questions might signify, "I don't know." Asking for help might mean, "I don't have the answer," and might incur the risk of appearing stupid or incapable. This is why navigating the fine line between speaking up and psychological safety can be difficult. We don't want to look incompetent. We don't want to admit to our mistakes or our weaknesses in front of others. But without being vulnerable, how is it possible to get the help we need to improve?

If you constantly strive *not* to look stupid, you are being selfish. How so? You are putting your need to look like the smartest person in the room ahead of your team's needs. That's not leading with vulnerability. The fear you create amongst the team inhibits their learning and consumes their valuable psychological resources. This impairs your team's problem-solving abilities as well as your ability to lead effectively.

If Autonomy means trusting your team and counting on them, psychological safety means your team trusts and counts on you. You don't want to create an army of followers who simply comply and disengage. You want to create an army of leaders who think for themselves.

> You want to create an army of leaders who think for themselves.

As leaders, we should be seeking to fail early and fail often, so we can quickly map a better way forward. We need to get comfortable with mistakes and failures. There is no room for perfectionism in psychologically safe high-performing teams. Therefore, we need people to speak up about mistakes and help us become aware of the things we don't see. The more frequently people speak up, the more we can learn about what's not working and correct it. This creates a higher-performing team connection and also stops excessive confidence (the Dunning-Kruger Effect) from setting in. What we want is excessive *competence*, not over-*confidence*, and what we need is higher performance—doing more of the stuff that drives performance and less of the stuff that doesn't. When this happens, everyone wins but your ego. Effective leadership is about seeking improvement in yourself via vulnerability, humility, and openness.

> "Vulnerability is not winning or losing; it's having the courage to show up and be seen when we have no control over the outcome. Vulnerability is not weakness; it's our greatest measure of courage." —Brené Brown[5]

A team that speaks up will let you know what you are doing both effectively and ineffectively, so you can do more of the former and less of the latter. This is your direct link to an improved version of yourself to lead your team. Humility leads to more engagement from your team, which leads to more learning, which leads to more Autonomy for everyone. And your team will love you for it.

START-STOP-CONTINUE EXERCISE

Ask yourself these start-stop-continue questions:

Start—*What am I not doing that I need to* start *doing, to bring more Autonomy to my team?*

Stop—*What am I currently doing that I need to* stop *doing, to bring more Autonomy to my team?*

Continue—*What am I currently doing that I should* continue *doing that is creating positive Autonomy for my team?*

Now we'll explore some of the cognitive biases that can prevent us from creating Autonomy on our teams. Have you ever been to IKEA? If not, we'll take you there in the next chapter.

CHAPTER 7

AUTONOMY BIAS #1
THE IKEA EFFECT

Ever notice that when you invest your labor and mindshare into putting something together—like, say, a piece of IKEA furniture—you feel a special connection to that piece? That can be a positive thing, but it can also cause you to assign too much mental value to an item or project, which can lead to skewed decisions in business.

The cognitive bias of our tendency to assign more value to something that we helped create is known as *the IKEA Effect*. The name refers to the Swedish furniture manufacturer and retailer, IKEA, which sells many items of furniture that require assembly. Basically, the more of your own effort you put into something, the more perceived value it has, and the more attached you become to it, even if there is a better option out there. You create attachment because your blood, sweat, and tears were put into it.

The IKEA Effect

I will never forget my first eureka moment regarding Autonomy and the IKEA Effect. DX Learning was embarking on building a new product. I already had in mind what needed to be done and how to go about it. Because I had been doing this stuff for many years and I was mentally invested in the methodologies I had learned through trial and error and through accumulated knowledge, I felt that I knew that the quickest, easiest way to build this new product would be *my* way.

But I had also just read *Quiet Leadership* by David Rock. So instead of telling people what to do during a design meeting, I decided to stay quiet. (Ask more, say less!) As usual, people were looking to me for answers, but this time I said, "How about you all spend the rest of the week thinking through ideas, and on Friday you present the best options?"

The look of excitement on their faces immediately told me I'd done the right thing. I sensed in that moment the immense power of Autonomy and realized I had been stealing it for years. The team was finally being given a project they felt was *theirs*. They were going to make the instruction manual the way *they* wanted it.

By the end of the week, the team had come up with ideas I never would have conceptualized—ideas that are still in play today in a product used by several Fortune 500 companies. The team broke through to new levels of creativity I would have stymied had we stuck to my original ideas. They believe in this product in a special way because they have ownership in its creation.

My story shows the IKEA Effect from both the negative and the positive sides. I was attached to my old way of doing things because I had invested years in developing my design principles; in doing so, I didn't want to let go of control. But by allowing the team to pour themselves into the new product design, I allowed the IKEA Effect to work in a positive way: everyone would now be much more invested in the new product.

The bias: We assign more value to something *we* helped to create.

The effect on Autonomy: On the upside, giving Autonomy to team members, so they "own" a project, results in more buy-in. On the downside, we are reluctant to give up ideas *we've* invested in, even if they're bad, which can rob our team of the Autonomy to try new things.

The cure: *Stop* assuming your way is the best way. *Start* allowing people the freedom to do things their way.

Using IKEA Every Day

When you make something by hand, you feel it's worth more than if someone else made the same thing. Just go on Etsy and look at all the overpriced arts-and-crafts projects. One of my neighbors did some renovations on their home and then put the house on the market. They substantially overvalued it because of their emotional attachment to the work they had done themselves. And Hollywood is full of screenwriters who expect to sell their first script for high six-figure fees, simply because they worked so hard on it.

Sometimes we price things based on the amount of time it took to make them—as well as on the investment we made learning the craft, buying the tools, etc. Many people, for example, think that making the mere effort to brush paint onto a canvas automatically gives their artwork as much value as a gallery piece. Same for a newly built home or a screenplay from a writer with multiple awards under their belt. But the market may beg to differ!

Even your resume may not be as amazing as you believe it to be. The fact that you spent hours working on it and found a beautiful template on Google doesn't mean your resume will necessarily rise to the top of the pile. (And BTW, just because you worked hard to organize a bake sale in high school doesn't mean you should still include it on your résumé at age forty-two).

If you're an entrepreneur, think of how much value you place on your business. It's your baby, I get it, but are you looking at it objectively? Is it being run efficiently and effectively? Could it be improved? Do you need more training, background, or experience to help bring it to the next level? Do you need to hire new people?

Sometimes we can become so attached to our current team or business, we're not always able to see where it could be made better or where it's faltering. And if given the feedback and insight to make it better, we may be unwilling to act on it because we spent so much of our own time and energy on it. We don't want to change anything, as it feels as if all that has gone to waste . . .

Your Brain on the IKEA Effect

The IKEA effect was identified and named by Michael I. Norton of Harvard Business School, Daniel Mochon of Yale, and Dan Ariely of Duke, who published the results of three studies in 2011. The first study found that subjects were willing to pay 63 percent more for furniture they had assembled themselves than for equivalent preassembled items. The other two studies showed similar tendencies to assign added value to items because of having worked on them.

"Labor alone can be sufficient to induce greater liking for the fruits of one's labor," noted the researchers. "[E]ven constructing a standardized bureau—an arduous, solitary task—can lead people to overvalue their (often poorly constructed) creations."[1]

This overvaluing of one's own work can lead to some serious distortions. "Participants saw their amateurish creations as similar in value to [an] experts' creations, and expected others to share their opinions."[2]

Of course, product designers and marketers have known about this bias for ages. Norton and his fellow researchers cited Build-a-Bear stores, which allow people to come into a "workshop" and make their own teddy bears. Many consumers enjoy this option, even though they are charged a high price for a product which, thanks to their free labor, allows the manufacturer to save on assembly costs. The researchers also pointed out the popularity of "Haycations" in which city people pay for the privilege of doing the farmers' work for them. Based on these cases and others, the researchers concluded that people are willing to pay a premium for items into which they have put a degree of their own labor.

When we build things by hand or put a lot of work into them, we tend to inflate their value cognitively because we add *personal value*. Our brains naturally think, "If I put all this time and effort into something, it must be worth something." This notion is what inflates the value to us. Because we were there for every screw turn, we know the piece was made well (or, at least, we *believe* that it was). And so, it becomes more valuable to us than if we bought it preassembled.

Now throw in the *sunk-cost fallacy*, whereby we tend to support items and ideas we've contributed to because, if they don't succeed, we'll be forced to recognize them as a waste of our time and resources.[3] Our brains don't want to accept that. So, we often argue, rather boisterously, for the value of our things and ideas that are not objectively the best option out there.

Here's another problem: we love to take *credit* for things that we have contributed value to. It's easy to overvalue our own contributions because work culture typically rewards and promotes people based on their ability to perform, which makes it tempting to take more credit than we actually deserve. We need to be aware of this tendency and keep it in check.

There's No Silver Lining in Sunk Costs

Years ago, my friend worked for a computer game company as a game designer. Buoyed by a few early successes, he and a group of creative teammates within the company decided to develop a children's game based on a completely original idea. They spent a lot of time and resources creating original characters, writing and designing the game, programming the game software, and developing a fully animated in-house demo.

When they excitedly showed the demo to the rest of the company, they were disappointed at the tepid reaction. "I don't get it" was the chief response by those who played it. The creative team was urged to drop the project, but because they had the authority to keep working on it, as well as the backing of one of the company's co-owners, they invested *more* of the company's resources in developing an *even larger* demo of the game.

When the larger, more polished demo was ready, they shared it with their mother company and a group of their publishing and distribution partners. Again, the response was not what they hoped for. "I don't get it" was the phrase that echoed around the conference room.

Convinced they were right and everyone else was wrong, they doubled down on their intention to develop the full game. At this point, however, they needed the backing of a large game publisher, and so they arranged a meeting with one of the world's biggest entertainment companies (its name rhymes with Fizz-knee). My friend and their team flew to California where they pitched the game to a room full of gaming executives. After the demo, they were asked to leave the room so the executives could confer. When the developers returned to the room a short while later, the chief executive delivered the verdict: "We really didn't get it, fellas."

The project was officially dead. Not only had they lost all the money sunk on developing the project, but they also lost the opportunity to do further projects with the big entertainment publisher; they were "disinvited" from pitching two other games they'd hoped to sell. And when the game company hit hard financial times a few months later, it had to shut down because it didn't reserve enough cash to keep going—the money had all been spent on the aborted game. The IKEA Effect blindsided my friend and his teammates.

Overcoming the Bias

So now that you know a bit more about this bias, why it arises, and how you can mess up with it, what should you do to keep it from creating imbalance in *your* life and leadership?

The first step is to recognize the IKEA Effect in your own leadership style. The IKEA Effect is particularly strong in entrepreneur-leaders, like me. Why? For years, we work our butts off on our fledgling business, and then we finally begin to reap some rewards. Convinced our work has merit and value, what do we do? We work even harder and keep our blinders on even tighter, so we stay laser-focused. But in doing all the work yourself, you don't have time to invite new feedback and perspectives, leading to tunnel vision.

And if you are doing all the work, who is not? Your team. By constantly doing more of the work, CAREless leaders take Autonomy away from their teams. They don't seek perspective or ask for feedback, and when they do, they ignore the input and go with their own decision. It's such a common, but illogical, tendency: they hire people for their skills and knowledge then turn them into worker bees for their own ideas.

> CAREless leaders take Autonomy away from their teams.

That's why it can be helpful to make structural changes to your decision-making and implementation processes, such as:

- **Stepping back and looking at your work processes.** Build in concrete checkpoints along the way for employees to contribute ideas to new initiatives and say when they think things aren't working. They'll feel some ownership in them and help you keep sunk costs at bay.
- **Gathering opinions.** Create feedback mechanisms that are meaningful and engaging. Remind yourself that even if your ideas are good, your team can make them better.
- **Meeting with key team members regularly.** This keeps your team active instead of passive and gives you time to listen, not lecture.

- **Rewarding team members for contributing ideas.** Recognize those who challenge the status quo and bring fresh ideas in team meetings. This will invite more ideas to come from those people and those who haven't spoken up yet.
- **Hiring a coach or advisor.** This will help you see when you are doing too much work and failing to share responsibility with your team.

CAREful leaders are all about empowerment. They don't do all the work for their team. They offer people a say in how things get done. They are crystal clear on what needs to be done (Clarity), but they grant the team the Autonomy for how to do it. They constantly ask the team, "What do *you* think about this?" Most importantly, they actually listen to their input. When the team makes mistakes, they allow them to learn from those mistakes without jumping in to solve problems. Even if they know the answer, they allow their team to find the answer for themselves.

Let's Work It

Conduct a process review with your team or teams. This can take place over a period of weeks or months. Look at each process you use in every department and ask your team to offer their feedback on that process. Create a safe space for them to be honest. Ask questions such as:

- Is this process the most effective and efficient one possible?
- How might it be improved?
- Should we replace it with a better process?
- Can technology help us improve this process?
- If we were starting a business from scratch, is this the process we would objectively use?
- What process do our competitors use? Is it working for them?

If changes are indicated, delegate team members to research new solutions. Put key team members in charge of implementing the new solutions. Give them the parameters, but let them figure out the details.

START-STOP-CONTINUE EXERCISE

Ask yourself these start-stop-continue questions:

Start—*What am I not doing that I need to* start *doing to reduce the IKEA Effect in my leadership?*

Stop—*What am I currently doing that I need to* stop *doing to reduce the IKEA Effect in my leadership?*

Continue—*What am I currently doing that I should* continue *doing that is keeping the IKEA Effect in check?*

As we've seen in this chapter, everyone needs to feel a sense of ownership over their projects. That only happens in an atmosphere of Autonomy. The next chapter takes Autonomy to another level. Ever been bitten by something nasty?

CHAPTER 8

AUTONOMY BIAS #2
ONCE BITTEN, TWICE SHY

One of the great things about Autonomy is that it offers us the freedom to make our own decisions and take our own risks, even though sometimes those decisions don't turn out how we planned. We learn by making mistakes. It just so happens that sometimes when we take a fall, the landing is a little harder than we anticipated, and we wrongly ascribe the failure to a factor that had little or nothing to do with the actual failure. We become hesitant to make that same choice again, even when it might be a perfectly good one.

Because we failed once already, we assume we will have the same outcome the next time we try. This is a cognitive bias known as Nonadaptive Choice Switching, also referred to as the Once Bitten, Twice Shy (OBTS) Bias.

Just like in the '70s hit song by Ian Hunter (later covered by the US glam band Great White), once we've been hurt by something, we are less likely to put ourselves in that same situation again. We tried it once and it led to a bad outcome, so we fear it will lead to the same bad outcome again. We don't like to feel regret; we also don't like to tempt loss. So, when a particular approach has caused loss in the past, we cross it off our options list for the future.

This bias is not good for creativity and innovation. It closes doors that could hold the key to growth and opportunity, and it closes minds. When we allow ourselves, as leaders, to fall prey to this bias, we rob our team members of options that might be fruitful, thus shrinking their Autonomy.

Once Bitten, Twice Shy

People often make declarations like, "Oh, I don't drink chardonnay," or "I don't eat sushi." For many, it's the "I will never drink tequila again," after a regrettable night in college. My brain has told me never to consume uni (sea urchin) again—even if starving on a desert island.

But there are great chardonnays. There are different kinds of sushi. Tequila can be enjoyed in many different ways. And I am sure not all sea urchin tastes like cleaning day at the shipyard. All this to say: just because something didn't work the first time doesn't mean it's a bad idea.

The bias: When a good decision leads to a bad outcome, we are less likely to select the same choice a second time, even when it is still objectively the best option.

The effect on Autonomy: Autonomy is all about learning from past mistakes, but sometimes we give too much weight to bad experiences.

The cure: *Stop* letting the past dictate the future. *Start* challenging your own assumptions.

Alexample: the Bias Machine

There are many stories of how this bias got the better of me, but this is one my team jokes about regularly. I'm glad *someone* finds this stuff amusing . . .

In order to be effective in our work, designing leadership-training experiences at DX, we leverage science to change behavior. So, hiring a scientific expert in the field of human behavior seemed like a no-brainer to me. I hired a PhD of industrial and organizational (I-O) psychology. For the purpose of this story, we'll call this person John.

When John and I worked together at DX, we achieved a lot. Having an expert on your team is a great opportunity for learning. I asked a lot of questions and got a lot of answers. Much of the philosophy and methodology of our business was formed during John's tenure.

But then we hit a few months of very soft revenue. The future suddenly didn't look as rosy as it once had. I took on debt for the first time to cover the growth of the business and shore up cash. I felt a strong need to take action on a couple of fronts. My usual "What do you think you should do this week?" approach turned to a "This is what we need to do this week."

As the CEO of a small business, my primary job is to ensure we make payroll. When I see finances in jeopardy, I *have* to make changes to address that. And I did. I dialed up Clarity and took back some of my team's Autonomy. As a leader, you give and take Clarity and Autonomy based on the situation and environment. But that whole

107

situation made me a little grittier than normal. John took me aside and told me what he thought about the situation and about me. His threat circuity had been triggered due to not having enough control (Autonomy) to feel safe. Fight-or-flight mode was engaged, and he chose to fight. He let his emotions get the better of him and said things neither of us would forget.

That was the turning point in our relationship. John *really* didn't like some of the changes I put in place, and, yes, I admittedly took some Autonomy away from him—at least temporarily. Our relationship was never the same after that, and he began resisting everything I tried to do. In the design of a new product, even when I clearly said, "This is not going to work," he still went ahead and did things his own way.

The experience did not end well, and John departed under a cloud of hard feelings. This led me to conclude that PhDs are lacking in EQ and don't have the right stuff to work in start-ups. *"John had an easily damaged ego; therefore, all people with PhDs have easily damageable egos"* was my thinking. I remember telling my wife (and anyone else who would listen), "I will never hire another PhD!"

But that was a narrow-minded, illogical reaction, and it really hindered me in the hiring process as we grew DX Learning. It was a fixed mindset, the opposite of the growth mindset we teach at DX—and the opposite of this book's message. How can a team feel psychologically safe if their boss behaves the way I did in this situation? I hope you can see how crazy it was to believe that the problems John and I had were *caused* by his degree. To allow myself to become biased in this way was to cut myself off from an enormously rich resource: people with PhDs. Though I'm not 100 percent there yet, I am working on controlling this bias. The experience left a terrible taste in my mouth. Every once in a while, John resurfaces on social media to issue a hate-rant about me, and the sour taste quickly returns.

But if I hadn't checked myself and my flawed assumption, I wouldn't have hired Sarah, who was set on achieving her PhD when we first met. I am grateful I didn't give into my biases and am lucky to have hired her. Sarah was very instrumental in putting together the research to help me write this book, and DX is now partnering with her to get her PhD in I-O psychology. I conquered my fear of Once Bitten, Twice Shy!

Studying the Bias

The phrase "Once bitten, twice shy" is often attributed to the ancient Greek storyteller Aesop as the moral of one of his fables. In the story, a wolf tries to eat a dog, but the dog convinces the wolf to hold off so he can fatten himself up first. The wolf agrees to come back later. When the wolf returns to the same spot and demands the dog give himself up, the dog wisely places himself well out of the wolf's reach. The wolf has learned his lesson.

This brings up an important point: the difference between an adaptive and a nonadaptive choice. In the fable, the dog makes an *adaptive* choice. He learns from past experience and makes a better choice the second time around. But what about when the choice is nonadaptive? That is to say, when the choice is stupid and uninformed?

Francesco Marcatto, Anna Cosulich, and Donatella Ferrante were researchers who devised a study on this bias. To summarize their study, they isolated a key factor that causes people to make nonadaptive choices: regret. In a rigged game of blackjack, the researchers created conditions whereby some of the test subjects failed to win a cash prize and regretted the way they had played their cards. In subsequent games, those who experienced regret on the first round were found to be more likely to make poor card choices in a second round than those who did not experience regret the first time around.

The researchers concluded that "When a good decision leads to a bad outcome, the experience of regret can bias subsequent choices: people are less likely to select the regret-producing alternative a second time, even when it is still objectively the best alternative."[1]

Humans are regret averse. We tend to avoid choices we associate with regretful outcomes. We would rather remain passive on a choice than actively pick something that may result in a regrettable scenario.

Humans are regret averse.

In 2005, psychologists Ratner and Herbst found more evidence for this effect. In their experiments, participants were asked to choose between two stockbrokers, one of whom had a better reported success rate than the other, and to make a small "investment." Obviously, most participants chose the broker with the better success rate. Half of them were then informed that this broker had succeeded with their investment; the other half were told that the broker had failed. All were then asked which of the two brokers they would choose the *next* time. Participants whose broker failed the first time regretted their decision and were less likely to select the same broker again, even though that broker still had the best overall success rate.[2] Nonadaptive behavior in play.

When leaders allow this bias to get in the way, it can be difficult to get them on board with change—even if it's change for the better. You might hear them say something like, "No, we've already tried that before," or "That just doesn't work in this company, trust me."

However, a more CAREful leader might look at the situation and say, "We tried that before, but we can definitely revisit it. Let's talk about what *specifically* didn't work and see how we might be able to alter that factor. Let's not make any assumptions here." They are open to giving the team the Autonomy to experiment, even if that means revisiting ideas that failed before and trying them in a new way. This is where Clarity comes in handy again, as well as your leader intuition, to know when to try something again or let it lie. Clarity helps give you the data to know what ideas to focus on, which to revisit/reopen, and what not to.

Once Bitten Here, Twice Shy There

The Once Bitten Bias pops up often without us even realizing it. For instance, we see it when parenting more than one sibling. If something didn't work with the first kid, we usually don't try it again with the other kids. However, this doesn't account for the fact that each of our kids is a completely different person, with his/her own needs, tendencies, and personalities.

Sometimes we decide we don't like a certain food, only to find out, years later, that we simply didn't like the way it was prepared the first time. It could have been that the sample itself was flawed. Have you ever had a bad oyster at a midwestern restaurant? Not exactly flown in fresh every day. But an oyster right out of the bay? Entirely different story.

We see this bias with people trying to break into the entertainment industry. A would-be actor has a bad audition—or maybe has a great audition but still doesn't land the part—and the bad experience causes them to crawl away with their tail between their legs and go back to making skinny soy lattes for working actors. "I'm never doing *that* again," they decide.

And here's another example from my seemingly bottomless business well. In the pre-COVID era, Grace, an employee, wanted to work remotely, but I always had it in my mind that "work from home" was just another way of saying, "Take the day off." This was based on a bad experience with a lazy team member. But I finally gave the idea another thought and offered Grace the Autonomy to work virtually, part-time, as long as she was getting results. To my surprise, she simply worked better from home. Grace became one of my top producers.

Overcoming the Bias

One of the best ways to overcome this bias is simply to understand regret and the role it plays. This is where self-awareness comes in handy. Whenever you hear yourself saying, "We tried that already and I don't want to get burned again," analyze your past choice objectively. Enlist the help of team members in doing this. Are you avoiding this choice for well-thought-out reasons, or is there a hidden bias at work?

Ask questions about what went *right* as well as what might not have worked so well. If possible, gather perspective from those who have had success with the approach that failed for you. Try to gain insight into what worked well for them, and see if you can reveal any blind spots you may have had. The situation could have been purely circumstantial or luck of the draw since two people can do the exact same process but only one fails at it. You can also hire a coach or consultant with specialized training in that area for another well-trained set of eyes and expertise on the situation.

As you think about moving forward with an initiative, ask yourself if your choices are motivated by seeking rewards or avoiding regret.

When we are motivated by potential reward, we are much more likely to make adaptive choices than when we are motivated by avoiding regret. As any competitive athlete will tell you, there is a huge difference between playing to win and playing not to lose. Try framing your decisions as reward-oriented rather than regret-oriented. The more crystal clear clarity we provide on the goals, expectations, and what winning really is, the more we can overcome this bias.

A great example of this is in the dating arena. Some people, after a bad breakup or nasty divorce, swear off dating and marriage forever. Their choice is regret-based. It is motivated by avoiding pain rather than seeking love and fulfilling companionship. They simply vow to "never go down that road again." But remember, it takes two to tango. If you had a dance partner who was constantly stepping on your toes, maybe your toes weren't moving out of the way fast enough! Maybe you were stepping with your right foot when it should have been your left.

Unless you look down at your own (metaphorical) feet to see what's actually causing all the toe-stomping, you may either end up with some pretty sore toes or you'll add dancing to the list of things you will "never try again." But let me tell you, life is so much better on the dance floor!

That doesn't mean that everything that goes wrong is ultimately your fault, but it does mean you were a participant. Blanket write-offs such as "PhDs are bad employees," "Leadership trainings are a waste of time," or "Hedge fund managers can't be trusted" are almost always myopic and facile. Usually, the situation that went wrong was complex and had multiple contributing factors. Try to analyze what really happened, including the role you might have played. Take the more adaptive route before simply rejecting a whole class of resources.

Here's a little tip: doing some research before you try something may prevent you from getting "bitten" in the first place. If you're trying something new for the first time—like oysters or training programs—make sure you're getting the highest-quality product and that it's being offered by someone who knows what they're doing. If you're going to reject something, reject it because you genuinely don't like it, not because it was a poor representation of what could have been a great experience.

Here are a few questions to consider when ruling out a past course of action:

- *What assumptions am I making by closing this door? Are they logical and realistic? Are other people having success with this approach? What might I be missing?*
- *Am I making a truly adaptive choice or a nonadaptive one?*
- *How do I really know my opinion to be true? How can I test my assumptions?*
- *Whom can I involve to double check that I am not letting my experiences get the better of me?*

Your team members can't have real Autonomy if you are limiting their choices based on your own bad experiences. And *you* can't have true Autonomy if you allow yourself to develop a fixed, negative mindset regarding options that could be helping you. Give you and your team back the Autonomy you deserve. Play to win; don't play *not* to lose.

Let's Work It

As a regular exercise, at least a few times a year, do a "postmortem" (or after-action review) of past business decisions—not just in the immediate aftermath but six months, one year, or two years later. Look back objectively at what you were trying to accomplish. Examine the choices you made. Consider the options you chose as well as those you didn't. What were your reasons for avoiding certain courses of action? Do those reasons hold up in hindsight?

When doing these reviews, follow these three steps:

1. Detach yourself from the situation. Look at it as if it was another company, or another team, making the decision and carrying it out.
2. Close your mouth! Open your ears. Get perspective from others.
3. Be open to any "findings"—even those showing it might have been you who caused the issues.

START-STOP-CONTINUE EXERCISE

Ask yourself these start-stop-continue questions:

Start—*What am I not doing that I need to* start *doing, to reduce the Once Bitten, Twice Shy Bias?*

Stop—*What am I currently doing that I need to* stop *doing, to reduce Once Bitten, Twice Shy?*

Continue—*What am I currently doing that I should* continue *doing that is keeping Once Bitten, Twice Shy in check?*

The world is evolving at an ever-increasing rate, and we need to evolve with it. We cannot be shy in how we lead our people, and we cannot shy away from ideas that could be what sets our team up so they can win. Don't let this bias get in the way of being the CAREing leader your team needs to get to higher performance.

ON AUTONOMY

Autonomy is all about giving a degree of freedom to those you serve so that your team can be at cognitive ease and free to produce in a relaxed, stress-free environment. Self-awareness is the key to controlling the cognitive IKEA Effect and Once Bitten, Twice Shy biases so that you can continue to build Autonomy within your team or organization.

Let go of your ego and stop trying to be in control. Give your team the keys so *they* can drive the bus. They may find a great new route—one you never considered. Don't be hasty to close the doors on them based on your own bad experiences.

Let go of the need to be a hero and helper. Let people fail within clear boundaries. Provide the walls of the box with Clarity and then turn people loose within the box. Trusting your team and giving them as much control as they need and as the situation permits will lead to psychological safety. Conversely, if your team senses you're taking control of things they can handle on their own, that will cause unnecessary stress.

Strive to avoid assuming. Ask more and tell less. Ask questions until your team feel entrusted to do what needs to get done on *their* terms. Don't let your brain tell you that just because *you* didn't build it (Ikea Effect) or just because it didn't work for *you* (Once Bitten, Twice Shy), it won't work for them.

Take my advice and just let go.

You'll know your team feels safe when they challenge you often. They'll freely come to you and tell you they're not comfortable with a decision or they suggest a better way of doing things. They don't accept being chained to how things are and they challenge the status quo—*that's* where higher performance comes from. You'll know they are *not* safe when there  is silence and everyone simply complies with your orders. In this case, you can be sure they are disengaged behind the scenes and on LinkedIn looking for a job.

CLARITY is the WHAT

AUTONOMY is the HOW

Clarity and Autonomy are joined at the hip. One does not work without the other. Not enough Clarity, and you will find it hard to give people the freedom they need—because you'll always be needing to recommunicate and rework, which will lead to your getting too involved. Too much Autonomy without enough Clarity feels like chaos to you and everyone around you. It's a fine line to dance between the two. When you get it right and give just enough of both, high performance can begin. It's the dichotomy and tension between the two that makes effective leadership so difficult. Every situation may require varying levels of one or the other. Get it wrong, and the team revolts and you spend your time fighting fires. Get it right, and the team will become resilient, self-sufficient, and fight their own fires, giving you more time to work on what comes next. Clarity and Autonomy work so interconnectedly that the varying degrees you give them to your team members will put their performance in varying zones. Those zones produce a certain kind of management, productivity, and culture style.

LOW C + LOW A = ANXIETY ZONE. You are in control, but there are no clear expectations on where the team is going. No team member wants to be here.

HIGH C + LOW A = MICROMANAGEMENT ZONE. Everyone is clear on where they're going, but it's "my way or the high way" mentality for you.

HIGH A + LOW C = CONFUSION AND CHAOS ZONE. Your team has the flexibility to make decisions, but there's no alignment on what the decision or expectations are.

HIGH A + HIGH C = HIGH-PERFORMANCE ZONE. Everyone knows what they need to do and can do it how it works for *them*. This is where you and your team perform to the best of their ability.

Which zone are you in? If you were to ask your team, their answer might be different. Where do you think they would put themselves? Probably a good conversation to have with your team tomorrow.

The key here is about movement. Where are you now, and how do you move closer to the top right. Every team and every situation are different.

Most leaders start close to the bottom left. Unfortunate, but true, even for me. When I started DX I had no choice. I was in control, not my team, and I had no idea where I was going! Since, I have been in all quadrants, finally closer to the top right, where I can achieve high performance and so can my team. I am not there yet, and I don't think you ever get to the top right, but it's the growth mindset of striving for that zone that will get you and your team closer to it. The key is to know where you are and create a plan to move the needle closer to the High-Performance Zone—where situational leadership is. It's important to get this balance between Clarity and Autonomy right before moving to the next part of the CARE Equation.

The next element of the CARE Equation, the "R" (Relationships), really gets to the heart of this playbook. The "C" and "A" steps are a rite of passage to ensure you have the time and attention to do the "R" right. So, are you ready for some magic?

PART III

Clarity

Autonomy

Relationships

Equity

CHAPTER 9

THE IMPORTANCE OF
RELATIONSHIPS

"I never knew that about you. Now it all makes sense!"

Leading is about connecting . . .

Leading is about connecting, but how can you connect to someone if you don't know what's important to them? How can you lead your people unless you know what makes them the human beings they are today? How can people believe you're working in their best interests if you don't know what those best interests are?

A whole lot of stuff is happening in people's lives—much of it more important than their jobs. Unless you know what that is, you can never lead them in a meaningful way. If you are not connecting with your people, you miss things that may be harming their well-being and the effectiveness of the whole team.

Clarity, as we have seen, is about providing a sense of mental certainty to your team so they can be at cognitive ease. Autonomy means giving up some control so that your people have a sense of freedom and investment that puts their brains at cognitive ease since they're in the driver's seat. The more Clarity and Autonomy you give your team, the better you are able to build Relationships.

Think about it: the more time you spend up front providing Clarity and Autonomy to your team, the less work you need to personally do on the back end and the more time you free up. This is time you can use to build Relationships. Many leaders are always on their back foot, fighting fires. That's because they haven't given their team sufficient Clarity and Autonomy. Thus, they have no time to get to know those they serve. They have no time to build Relationships. And it's the Relationships that matter more than anything else.

By building Relationships, I don't mean just hanging out with people and shooting the breeze. I mean trying to understand how their lives and experiences molded them into the human beings that come to work with you every day. It's actively striving to know, not assume, what these people require to be fully engaged and performing at their best. Doing relational work enables you to lead your team with a personalized approach that removes physical and emotional barriers that may be getting in their, and your, way.

Putting People First

A couple of years ago, one of my team members adopted a child. It was at a time when I was deep in the weeds, working on pivoting the business to a new model for a new world. It was also a time when we were all working remotely, due to COVID. My head was down, doing the work. So, if my head was down, where was my head not? Above the work and focusing on my people.

When I finally started doing one-on-ones again—where I get to ask people nonwork questions—I learned that this team member had not had daycare on Tuesdays. So, for three months, she'd been looking after her new child while doing the same amount of work as before. I was in shock and immediately saw the consequences of my failure to connect. If I had known about her childcare situation, I could have ensured that the team refrained from communicating with her on Tuesdays. I could have given her half a day off. Whatever it was she needed to do her job and care for her child, I could have done *something* more than nothing-at-all to make her life easier. I realized I was operating under the "No news is good news" and assuming everyone was okay because I wasn't hearing any differently. That's on me because I wasn't making time for myself to be available to *hear* anything different.

For the sake of this playbook, let's define Relationship as *demonstrating you care about your team by connecting* with *your team on a human level.* That means changing your focus from results-first to people-first. When you put people first and results second, you end up fostering a team that creates the best results anyway—far better than when you put results first. It's a vast oversimplification, but it's basically true in the long run: When you put people ahead of results, you get both. When you put results ahead of people, you get neither.

> Relationship [is] demonstrating you care about your team by connecting with your team on a human level.

125

At DX, my people *always* come first. I place great value on how I treat them, and that treatment is informed by getting to know them on a personal level and understanding what's going on in their lives. I put a high premium on trust (Autonomy), and I try to build that trust by showing that I care through actually CAREing, connecting, listening, and maintaining a bond with people. Not only is this human connection intrinsically rewarding, but it also gives me insight into people's aspirations and dreams, both work and nonwork. I get to know what matters most to them, what fun means to them, how they want to live their lives, and where they want to live. Even what they like and don't like about me, I get to know that too! This allows me to tailor how I lead them to their preferences—not mine. And they become a happier, more satisfied team with higher performance levels.

It's a Survival Thing

The brain is wired to place great importance on establishing, securing, and maintaining bonds with others. There's an inborn need for human connection and trust. We humans are "pack animals" (i.e., social creatures). In our early days as a species, we were much more likely to survive if we were part of a tribe. A sense of belonging, connection, and contributing value meant *"I am needed by the tribe; I have a sense of worth here."* If we were exiled or if we weren't valued in some way, our survival would be threatened. We'd be left out in the cold, trying to make it on our own with no one to help us keep watch or defend ourselves. We would likely be killed by a predator or die of exhaustion or starvation. Relationships, therefore, have immense survival value to our brains.

There are also emotional, and for some, spiritual, reasons we crave Relationships. We are all part of the fabric of humanity. We naturally seek to have that connection reinforced and to share love, laughter, and caring with others. Relationships are what give meaning and joy to life, and it is unnatural for us to cut ourselves off from that connection.

There's a great book and later film about this concept called *Into the Wild.* It's the true story of Christopher McCandless, also known by his pseudonym Alexander Supertramp, who wanted to prove to himself and society that he would be happier living in seclusion in the Alaskan wilderness. After abandoning his car, burning his IDs, and even burning his cash, he took his few remaining possessions and headed for Alaska. By the time he made it "into the wild," he found himself less prepared than he thought. Due to late snow and dangerous river levels, he became stranded on an inlet with limited resources. He survived for 113 days on squirrels, birds, roots, and seeds until he ate a poisonous plant and starved himself to death.

His body was eventually found by a hunter in the abandoned bus he used for shelter. There he inscribed on the wall one final regret: "Happiness [is] only real when shared."

The business landscape is littered with examples of people who put results ahead of people and either failed because of it or managed to succeed only to later regret their Scrooge-like ways. No one on their deathbed ever says, "I wish I had valued money more and people less." No one. I'm not trying to be preachy or moralistic here; I'm just saying that it's good to remind ourselves from time to time that people are the whole reason we do what we do.

Relationships are *why* we do what we do and *how* we do what we do. On our best days, nothing feels better than sharing our successes with our team and those we care about. And on our sh*t days, nothing feels better than to have someone lift us up, be a beacon of light, and give us the encouragement that tomorrow will be a better day. When everyone feels valued for who they are, everyone brings their fullest selves and their best selves to work every day. And you get engagement at the highest level—which is great for business.

Engagement Flows from Relationships

Employee engagement drives success, so it's only natural that the companies who engender high employee engagement are those that emphasize human connection and create a people-first culture for their employees. It's a mentality that starts at the top. As leaders, we don't need to be best friends with everyone, but we do need to forge genuine human connections throughout the company. Leaders also need to remember that your team is not your family. Your family is your family. Your responsibility to your team is to treat them as the humans they are and build an environment that allows them to do their best work and be their best selves.

A September 2020 article posted by McKinsey & Company, "The Boss Factor: Making the World Better Through Workplace Relationships," states, "When it comes to employee happiness, bosses and supervisors play a bigger role than one might guess. Relationships with management are the top factor in employees' job satisfaction." *The top factor.* A Gallup statistic that has been reinforced by other polls reveals that an employee's perception of their manager accounts for a 70 percent variance in their engagement level.

On the flip side, a survey quoted in a September 2018 issue of the *Harvard Business Review* states that "75 percent of survey participants said that the most stressful aspect of their job was their immediate boss."[1]

In short, when you are "the boss," you play a huge part in setting the happiness and stress levels of your team. How do you ensure that you're *enhancing* job engagement rather than damaging it? By becoming a shining example of someone who is CAREful and selfless—someone who invests in Relationships. Let's look at a few key ways you can do that.

Learn to listen: conversation is about them, not you

Have you ever worked for someone who constantly relates the conversation to their own experiences, interrupts regularly, and circles any question they ask back to themselves? Someone who is always talking more than everyone else? This trait is what is known as *conversational narcissism.* It is driven by a need to be liked and to connect. Human brains, after all, crave acceptance. A feeling of being disliked triggers the survival fear of being left out of the tribe. So they go into overdrive and talk themselves up.

But ironically, the real way to connect is to listen to others. Everyone loves a listener.

Keep yourself out of the picture. Regard every interaction as an opportunity to discover who the people around you are and what is important to *them*. The less you talk about *you* and the more you listen to others, the greater value you have to the "tribe" that you're creating in your company. Leading can kind of be like a therapist-patient relationship. You need to be close to people to offer them help, but your relationship may not be as effective if your team knows all your personal sh*t in detail. As a leader, you should always aim to know more about your team than they know about you, which means you need to listen more than you talk.

Check in with yourself as you're speaking. How often do you use the word "I"? When you catch yourself talking about you, shift the conversation back to the other person (or people) by asking a question, and then actually listen to the answers you receive. And when you see the other person trying to speak, yield the floor to them and stop talking.

Check in with yourself as you're listening too. Are you waiting, maybe a bit too eagerly, for your turn to speak? Thinking about what you want to say next? When you catch yourself doing this, shift your full attention to the person speaking. This simple shift of attention will do more to create Relationships than all the books and workshops in the world can. Listening is the secret sauce of Relationships and is, therefore, an essential part of becoming an effective leader.

> Listening is the secret sauce of Relationships . . .

A Tale of Two Bosses

Before I founded DX, I was building and running the US office of a UK-based employer. I had two very different bosses and two drastically different experiences. We'll call them Paul and Diane. Most conversations with Paul centered around his experiences at a large corporation and how he made lots of money and won award after award. He was always telling me what to do based on how *he* had done things. Paul had little empathy for me in my role, which was running a suboffice of an entrepreneurial organization during a global recession.

I rarely felt heard by Paul and came away from most conversations with a feeling of anger and disgust. I was cognitively stressed *all* the time. Paul couldn't relate to where I was at, nor could he help me. How could he when he was constantly filling in the gaps in our conversations with his own experiences rather than empathizing with mine? My needs were rarely met, I felt belittled, and my performance was at an all-time low. Paul was released by the company, but the damage was done. The experience left emotional scars.

Fortunately, I had the opposite experience with Diane. She always led conversations in an open and honest way that allowed space for me to talk. She would ask follow-up questions and then tie in relatable experiences so I could connect the dots and create new synaptic connections.

Conversations with Diane often started with "Talk to me more about X . . ." and then there would typically be a "How does that make you feel?" or "So what you're saying is . . ." or "Have you thought about doing X?" Then she would say, "Let me help you. Here is a situation I faced that relates to what you're saying." With Diane I always felt heard. I had a voice that mattered. She met me where I was at without judgment. Under her, my performance improved year after year.

In hindsight, I don't blame Paul. I have empathy for him. The human brain wants to forge connections and we do it the best way we know how, at whatever consciousness level we are at. For him, talking about his past successes was perceived to be seen as knowledgeable and impressive, which in his mind would make me feel confident with him as an effective leader even though, in my mind, it didn't. I never told him how his behaviors made me feel. He never knew about his leadership gaps because I was afraid of the consequences of giving him feedback. Because I lacked the control I craved, my threat circuitry was constantly triggered, and I did not feel psychologically safe. So, I remained silent. More self-awareness would have helped us both.

Silence kills business. Silence kills leadership. Silence kills relationships.

Some steps to follow

Here are a few steps to help you fight conversational narcissism and practice real listening:

1. **Start each conversation with an open-ended question.** That's a question designed to get the other person talking, not one that can be answered with a one-word reply. Start with phrases like, "Tell me about . . ." or "How do you feel about . . ." or "What are your thoughts on . . ."

2. **Listen when others are talking.** Turn off thoughts of your own experiences. Perhaps take notes on what the other person is saying.

3. **Talk less.** Monitor how much you talk versus others. Strive for a 70/30 ratio where you listen *at least* 70 percent of the time and talk 30 percent of the time *at most*.

4. **Ask follow-up questions.** "I haven't been in that situation; could you say more?" or "What else?" or "How did that make you feel?" Always dig deeper and try to find out if the person has more to say on the topic. One question is never enough.

5. **Sum up the conversation and ask if you missed anything.** This creates relational clarity, which only improves relationships as you build alignment.

Notice that not once in these steps do you talk about your own experiences because *that's not your job.* Relationships develop and strengthen by listening to others. That means turning off your internal wiring and your need to dominate conversations. Ask questions. Listen to the answers without interjecting. Ask clarifying questions to make sure you're understanding the person. Let them know you actually *hear* what they're saying. Ask how you can support them, and, when appropriate, inject some empathy or compassion about their situation.

Going back to the "Remember your best boss" from the beginning of the book, it was all relationship-based answers. Relationships dictate how you feel about someone and can be the tipping point between having an excellent team member who has your back or them finding a place that will make them feel better than they do now.

Remember that Everyone is Different

Something to consider in trying to create meaningful Relationships is that not everyone has the same needs or tendencies. Some people are very chatty, open, and intimate about their lives, like me. I can talk about nonwork stuff all day. And then there are the more operational people who just love to get down to business. Some people thrive in meetings and social situations. Others shrink.

No one's reaction is right. And no one's wrong either. People have different needs and preferences. The important thing is to make some time available to meet people's needs where *they* are at. Try to understand the various personality types among your team members, so that you can make adjustments as necessary. We all have a tendency to assume that everyone is basically just like us. We often assume we all have the same social needs, the same cognitive processing habits, and the same fears and insecurities as we do. But that usually isn't true. Although we all share a vast amount of common human ground, we are quite different in many ways.

As a leader, it is highly beneficial to make conscious efforts to understand the personality of each of your team members. The best way to do this is simply to ask. *Do you consider yourself more introverted or more extroverted? Do you like external structure or are you more of an independent producer? What's your conflict-resolution style? Are you task-oriented or people-oriented?* Your people aren't replicas of you, and you don't need a bunch of mini-you's. They have different requirements and different approaches to work, problem-solving, and life in general. That's the beauty of working with other people: different strengths interact and lead to more dimensional problem-solving which yields better results—if you know what those are and know how to use your team member's talent effectively.

The bottom line is not to make assumptions. An employee who seems aloof might actually be insecure or going through something at home. A social situation, such as an office party, might be rewarding for some employees but stressful for others—some people *gain* energy from interacting with others; others are drained by the same experience. Different personality types respond to situations in different ways. Never assume you know what is going on. To know is to not assume.

Find out about people's work preferences

Spend some of your one-on-one time with staff members trying to better understand their work habits and preferences and what you can do to support them. Without sounding like you're grilling them in a job interview, ask questions like:

1. **What do you consider your greatest skills and weaknesses?** This invites areas for them to feel confident, and you give feedback on why you feel the same, or indifferent, and where you've seen them excel. When they open up about where they feel weak in, approach it as a chance for self-awareness and improvement. Mention your weaknesses first to make them feel okay with vulnerability. Don't belittle them or say that because they can't do it now, they never can. Encourage them and discuss ways you can help them grow.

2. **What can I do to help you succeed and do your best work?** This will give you an idea of their working style and what they need to feel at ease in the workplace. Maybe they need to be surrounded by other people so there's camaraderie, or they need to be more isolated. A mixture. If they need specific tools and it's in your power to get them, find a way you can make that a part of their day-to-day work so that they can grow and be more efficient. It will ultimately pay you back in the long run. Schedules, due dates, and expectations could also be items that they need to feel comfortable before moving forward on a project.

3. **What do you like/dislike about your current role?** You may be opening a can of worms with this one, but do it anyway. Hear what they enjoy, and make sure to keep this stable for them; as for what they don't enjoy, hear why, and understand their point of view on the matter. Provide opportunities for them to learn more about why the area that they dislike is key to the operation, or if it isn't, see if you can delegate it to someone else. Ask about career goals and if there is any room in their current role that can help them get closer to it.

4. **What motivates and inspires you?** Find out their motivations, personal missions, and how their job works for their passions and personal interests. Knowing, and acting, the way they like

to be praised or rewarded for what they do also shows that you are listening and value them as a team member.

5. **What don't I know about you as a person, not an employee, would improve the way we connect and improve our working relationship?** This gives them the options to tell you about what makes them tick. You'll be getting "data" from them on what is going on behind the scenes so you can better engage with them and meet them where they are at.

Find out about people's nonwork lives

It's equally important to have some insight about who people are outside of work. You will learn a lot about them just by having unstructured "How's life?" conversations. But some people are more reticent about personal information than others. Taking care not to be too prying or violating boundaries, it sometimes helps to ask specific questions, such as:

1. **What are your passions and interests?** Maybe they enjoy reading, watching movies, or they are a huge sports fan. This can also give you two something to connect about on the day-to-day.

2. **What's a great day entail for you?** This will give you an idea of what they hold important outside of work, any interests they have, relationships outside of work that are important to them, and what they like to do in their spare time.

3. **What do you want people to know about you?** It might be an odd question at first, but this will invite them to share with you how they want to appear, what they are like, and what they hold important to themselves.

4. **What is one goal you would like to accomplish this year outside of work?** Most everyone has a dream or aspiration, and often, those aren't career based! Showing an interest in how they grow in their personal time will show them you value their efforts and dreams, and it might even give you an idea for how to put that skill set to work in the future.

If your team feels psychologically safe with you as their leader and in their working environment, they will be more receptive to opening up to you about their personal lives, which will make these questions and conversations flow a lot easier. But if you have not created psychological safety and you suddenly switch your leadership style, people may think it's a trap and you're looking for vulnerabilities to exploit. Persist. CARE. Psychological safety doesn't happen overnight.

Hang out together

Do things with your team members outside the normal scope of work. Set aside time for walk-and-talks and team-building days/exercises (recognizing that some people *hate* such things). Even social activities outside of work will do the trick. Try to build bonds and just have fun once in a while. Go out to lunch or dinner together. End work early and have a cookout. Spend a day together at a museum, an aquarium, or an amusement park. Laugh, have fun, and let your guard down a bit. The connections and synergy this builds among your team members will get you through those times of stress and higher workloads.

Be vulnerable

When trying to build relationships, don't be afraid to be vulnerable. Vulnerability is not weakness; it is strength. It takes courage to be vulnerable, but it will help others find their own voice and be vulnerable when *they* need to be. We can't help people unless they ask for help. And people will not ask for help in an atmosphere of "Let's all pretend we're perfect." Brené Brown's TED Talk, "The Power of Vulnerability," remains the fourth most viewed TED Talk worldwide. In it, Brown draws a connection between your willingness to ask for help and your ability to support others. If you berate yourself whenever you need help, you're unconsciously berating those who come to you for assistance. However, by accepting your own vulnerability and modeling it for others, you say that it is okay to need help. You provide a psychological safety net. Helping others takes courage and compassion, but it takes even more courage and compassion to accept help for yourself.

> Vulnerability is not weakness . . .

135

When people are in a place where they have worked hard to create psychological safety, the result is respectful, open conversations. People can be honest about their disagreements and say what needs to be said, knowing others won't hold it against them. They can argue, debate, and even get a bit angry with one another, but they will go home feeling complete knowing that they said what they needed to say and bearing no grudges.

Speaking of which . . .

Don't leave things unsaid

Many times, I have finished work and had the chance to give a team member feedback on something they did that day, but I chose not to say anything. What typically happens next is that I continue to think about it. My brain makes up things about that person that are not true. *"They didn't send me that report at five o'clock as they said they would. They must be lazy or irresponsible."* I then become emotional and fail to be present for my family because of this unfinished business that is eating away at me. A grudge starts to form. The next morning, I can't control my biased brain, and I say something regrettable to the team member.

All it would have taken was a phone call the previous day.

"Hey, you promised this report by five. I don't have it. What's going on?"

"My daughter was sick, and I had to take her to the doctor. I never got a chance to call you."

Not lazy. Not irresponsible. And I did not have a nice evening with my family because I spoiled it over incomplete communications.

Tend to your home relationships too

Establishing relationships at work are vital, but you still need to tend to your nonwork relationships as well. If you're having unresolved problems at home, you're likely to find yourself transferring those same issues to your team members and employees. And if you've had a sh*t day at the office, it is very easy to bring that sh*t energy home to your families and friends.

Try to keep your relationships clean and vibrant, both inside and outside the office. All the tips in this chapter can be applied to improve your relationships on the home front as well. Make time for friends, families, spouses, and neighbors. Whenever possible, try to include these people in your work environment. Consider hosting events where your work relationships and personal relationships can intermingle.

All your relationships, together, make up the fabric of your life. And you are at the center of this fabric. Let everyone see the real you so that you don't have to hide aspects of yourself. Don't take yourself so seriously. Have a sense of humor. Let people joke about you. This will not detract from your "status" as a leader. Rather, it will create stronger bonds amongst all the relationships in your life.

And don't forget to tend your relationship with *yourself!* There's a saying that if *you* don't like the person in the mirror, how do you expect anyone else to? Healthy relationships with others start with your relationship with yourself. If there is something you don't accept in yourself, you won't accept it in others—you will be harshly critical of people who exhibit that trait, and other people may be harshly critical of it in you too. So you really have a duty to your team (and family) to become self-aware and self-accepting.

START-STOP-CONTINUE EXERCISE

Ask yourself these start-stop-continue questions:

Start—*What am I not doing that I need to* start *doing, to build stronger relationships with my team?*

Stop—*What am I currently doing that I need to* stop *doing, to build stronger relationships with my team?*

Continue—*What am I currently doing that I should* continue *doing, to build stronger relationships with my team?*

Next, we'll look at Illicit Transference—one of two big cognitive biases that can affect Relationships.

CHAPTER 10

RELATIONSHIP BIAS #1
ILLICIT TRANSFERENCE

As a British guy living in America, I have been on the receiving end of this next bias a number of times, and I can tell you it is annoying. "Are you from London?" people tirelessly ask me. *No, not everyone from the UK was born in London. Why don't you ask me where I was born instead of assuming we're all from London!* "How bad are your teeth?" *Pretty good actually. No, we don't all have bad teeth.*

Making assumptions can be more than annoying though; it can really damage Relationships and undermine psychological safety and performance. This is the cognitive bias known as Illicit Transference, and it's one of the two biases that keep us from making the relationships needed to sustain psychological safety and for the CARE Equation to succeed.

Illicit Transference

Like most people, I'd be lying if I said I never generalized—that I don't sometimes categorize people based on limited information.

For example, in the early days of DX Learning Solutions, there was one industry I could just not crack: finance. Try as I might, I *never* got a yes, or even a whiff of a yes, from the finance industry. Based on this experience and coupled with what I had read in industry magazines and picked up from the general culture, I began to think of the finance industry as just a bunch of a**holes interested in one thing—money. This generalization led me to say, "We don't work with the finance industry." This mindset nearly cost me dearly when the chance to work with a particular client in the finance industry presented itself to DX. My brain was saying, *"Just move on, this is a waste of time, effort, and money."* My heart said, *"Slow down, look into this more."*

Luckily, I listened to my heart, and this finance company is now one of our biggest clients, and I count many of the people who work there as friends. They are definitely not a**holes, nor are they interested in only one thing. I was wrong.

The bias: We assume that attributes of a group apply to each individual in the group and that attributes of an individual apply to the whole group.

The effect on Relationships: We tend to stereotype people, which causes us to seek or avoid relationships with people for groundless reasons.

The cure: *Stop* stereotyping and generalizing based on nothing but your assumptions. *Start* getting to know people for the humans they are.

Examining the Bias

The Illicit Transference Bias is an umbrella name for two logical fallacies: the *fallacy of composition* and the *fallacy of division*.

The fallacy of composition is the false assumption that *what is true of a part is true of the whole*. We observe a specific trait in a person then generalize it to an entire group. For example: *Since Kathy, a MicroCorp employee, was honest with me in our transactions, I assume MicroCorp is a trustworthy company.* The fallacy of division is the reverse. It is the assumption that *what is true of the whole is true of each individual part*. For example: *MegaCorp was recently sued for fraud; therefore, every MegaCorp employee is dishonest.*

These two fallacies are known together as Illicit Transference—the idea that you can generalize attributes from the group to the individual or from the individual to the group. This bias often combines with other false generalizations to further distort the truth. *Generation Z (Gen Z) are entitled jerks. Tom is Gen Z. Therefore, Tom is an entitled jerk.* Here, even the foundational premise, "Gen Z are entitled jerks," is based on a flawed generalization. When we then apply it to an individual, its connection to the truth becomes even more strained.

Illicit Transference gets in the way of building diverse, trustful, and respectful relationships in all areas of life, not just work. My wife was cheated on by a former boyfriend, and to this day she has trust issues with men, which can create relational problems between us.

What we're really talking about here is stereotyping. Making sweeping generalizations, perceiving trends—perhaps inaccurately—and then applying them to individuals. In social psychology, a stereotype is a fixed, overgeneralized belief about a particular group or class of people. When we stereotype, we assume a person has a whole range of characteristics that we also assume the group possesses (a double assumption). We have all done this, just as we have all been generalized about or put into a category we didn't necessarily belong in. Racism, agism, sexism—these are all examples of Illicit Transference.

Stereotypes are usually thought of as negative preconceptions, but they can swing the other way too. We can falsely assume that people have positive qualities simply because they belong to a certain group, like people often assuming I'm smart *because* I have a British accent, or that the whole group has positive attributes based on our experience with one individual. This can end in disastrous consequences for *you*, even if you don't offend the person you're stereotyping. Retail businesses are well aware of this tendency. They know that a customer's good experience with a service representative will cause that customer to think well of the entire company; a bad experience will do the opposite.

Alexample on Illicit Transference

For a few years, I generalized in an insidious way that kept me from connecting to people on an individual level. It stemmed from my experience with a team member—we'll call him Jim—who moved from Chicago (where our office is) to Minneapolis and thereby became a remote employee. This did not work out. A big reason was that I'm not good at managing virtual people. "Out of sight, out of mind" is my tendency (which I am working to correct). I prefer the live company of people. This is neither right nor wrong; it's just my preference. When Jim became virtual, I had trouble pinning him down. Tasks were not being completed, and he was unreliable in his presence and availability. His production level dropped. I didn't trust that he was working full-time and giving us his best.

Because of this bad experience with Jim, I adopted a negative feeling toward *anyone* who wanted to work remotely. When another team member—a reliable person—asked me to work from home, my immediate take was that she wanted to coast. And when I did start grudgingly allowing telecommuting, I could still feel myself connecting more to the people in the office than those who worked from home. This hindered relationships with certain individuals. Most of the people who wanted to work from home were younger, which only compounded the problem. Now my brain began assuming that *all young people* were looking for the easy route. *Maybe I should hire more people like me! That will be better for team cohesiveness!*

Luckily, the pandemic forced me to blow up all my preconceived ideas about remote work and gave me a new toolbox for connecting with people who are not in the office. I am now better equipped to battle this bias in myself and to ensure I have strong relationships with all those I serve, no matter where they are located. I also have a revamped business model that's better suited for today's demands, and remote work allows me the flexibility to expand my team with high-quality people, even if I don't get to hug them on a regular basis (which they might consider a plus).

The IT (Illicit Transference) Team

I asked my team to come up with some stereotypes or generalizations that they had encountered in their lives. I'm sure you can think of plenty more.

- *All white people are lactose intolerant.*
- *All British people love tea and crumpets.*
- *All [insert a sports team from any city] fans are rude idiots.*
- *Introverts are shy, quiet, and reserved.*
- *Extroverts are loud, obnoxious party animals.*
- *Asian Americans are good at math.*
- *Germans are humorless and precision oriented.*
- *BMW drivers are inconsiderate.*
- *Women are worse drivers than men.*
- *Millennials are lazy and want things handed to them.*
- *If you're a woman over forty with more than two cats, you are a "crazy cat lady."*
- *Pitbulls are dangerous attack dogs.*

The list goes on. And on. And on.

CARE to Win

And the effects of Illicit Transference can be deeply harmful. Think of the way Muslims have been treated in the aftermath of 9/11. Or the way black drivers have been targeted by police at a higher rate than white people. One that really annoys me is that young people from Generation Z "don't want to work hard." These are all wrong and assumptive.

One of the great privileges I had growing up was the amount of travel I did for school and later for work. Travel is a great way to limit the IT Bias because it exposes you to people from so many different walks of life. As you are exposed to all that exists in our world, learning to accept differences becomes almost second nature. I truly believe that the more you travel and experience diverse cultures and lifestyles, the more inclusivity and empathy you build. Of course, we don't all have the luxury to travel, but we can be exposed to different thoughts and people in our workplaces and personal, everyday lives too. I have worked to ensure my friends are from varied cultural backgrounds and to expose myself to a wide range of points of view. I try to hire people who are very much unlike me in order to maintain a balance of perspective and a diversity of thought.

However, this still doesn't cure the problem entirely. Nor does it prevent the Illicit Transference Bias from being used on *you*.

Your Brain on Stereotypes

We make assumptions based on trends we perceive and then apply them to populations or individuals for ease of categorization. It's practical for the brain to put things into labeled boxes and then pull that information up when we need it. This is known as *schema theory*, which states that all human knowledge is organized into units. Within these units of knowledge, or *schemas*, information and memories are stored.

Schemas allow us to quickly access information so we can use it for making practical, moment-by-moment decisions. When we create a "schema" for a concept, we essentially create a file that contains all the ideas, sense-related data, and information we connect to that concept. For example, your schema for "picnic" may contain general information about what the word means. It will also contain memories, good or bad, of picnics you experienced as a child, along with sensory details such as the smell of pine trees, the taste of tuna salad sandwiches, and the feel of sunshine on your skin. For example, *my* schema of a picnic is a happy scene with my wife and kids sitting round an amazingly prepared menu of food items and drinks my wife has prepared, ready to watch a movie outside on a big screen. For someone else, their schema could be the horror of sand-infested sandwiches and seagulls trying to steal things. A schema thus represents both our conscious and unconscious knowledge about concepts. When we tap into a schema about an object or concept, we unlock its relationship with other objects, situations, events, and actions.

Our brains naturally employ this system for categorizing things. But when we use this same system to categorize *people*, we are falling victim to stereotyping and prejudice. People are not things or ideas. They are complex, multidimensional, and unique.

Just because someone is Indian doesn't mean they can cook curry.

Just because someone is tall doesn't mean they like playing basketball.

Just because someone is an introvert doesn't mean they don't like parties.

It's easy to see how using schema theory on people can be a problem both inside and outside of a work environment. For example, Google has long promoted a culture of openness, but a few years ago it faced harsh criticism around its hiring and promoting of women and minorities. In 2017, one of Google's software engineers was fired for an internal memo that rationalized the gender gap in the tech industry based on certain stereotypes such as that women were less interested in high-stress jobs because they were more anxious. The memo spread like wildfire throughout Silicon Valley, and Google had its hands full putting out the fire.

Striving to eliminate discrimination and human-rights violations is a social focus that goes far beyond the workplace. One kind of stereotype that has been particularly harmful to society is racial bias. Negative beliefs about black people have often been carried from one white generation to the next, without the "carriers" even knowing where the belief comes from.

The problem with using schemas on people is that people don't fall into neat buckets that easily define them. Every quality of every individual is on a spectrum, and these spectra don't line up the same way for any two people on Earth. Every person is an individual with their own strengths, weaknesses, preferences, and perspectives.

> Every person is an individual with their own strengths, weaknesses, preferences, and perspectives.

Overcoming the Bias

How do we overcome this bias and create fresh Relationships that carry no excess baggage? It isn't easy to root out unconscious beliefs. Why? Because they are, after all, unconscious. But it *can* be done . . . with commitment and consistent effort.

Part of being a leader (and a responsible adult) is to perform a thorough inventory of the beliefs you were brought up with regarding other people and to either discard them, enrich them, or replace them with more empowering ones. If you stay fixed in the beliefs you learned growing up, they will continue to create Relationship limitations for the rest of your life. This is not only unfair to *you* but also to everyone you might potentially work with. I say "potentially work with" because your stereotypes might cause you to not hire someone in the first place—someone who could potentially be a great asset to your team.

> Make a practice of meeting people where they are at . . .

Make a practice of meeting people where they are at, without prejudgment. Don't view them as members of any group; take them for who they are. To stereotype and generalize is to judge. To meet people where they are is to look underneath the surface and see their strengths, preferences, perspectives, and the pure, shining light of their humanity.

How well do you really know your team? Do you know them primarily as individuals or do you think of them as representatives of various demographics? Give that question some serious thought. Review the advice in the last chapter. Spend some time getting to know your people beyond just work conversations and general chitchat. Ask questions about their background, family, interests, and try to root out any assumptions you might be making. Look for what makes them unique, not what makes them similar to others in their respective categories.

It's possible to overcome prejudice and judgment when you listen more than you talk. Encourage regular discussions to explore employee diversity in terms of generational differences, work styles, philosophy, and ethics. Avoid making assumptions, but rather, ask your team to fill in the blanks for you. If you aren't sure about something, ask! (But also, don't burden others with the responsibility of educating you on things you can easily learn on the Web.) The more you ask and the more you listen, the more cared for they will feel and the more they will care back. And when the time is right, be willing to share openly about yourself as well.

As a leader, you have a responsibility to maintain fair employment practices and to treat members of your team fairly, regardless of race, gender, age, or any other category. Try to increase diversity and awareness on your team by creating opportunities for people to collaborate with others from different backgrounds, genders, and ages.

Let's Work It

Quickly write 3-5 traits about millennials (born after 1980).

Now write 3-5 traits about boomers (born from 1945-1964).

After you have written both descriptions out, look at the profiles below.

Millennial profile: Kendra works at the corporate headquarters for a multinational organization in Raleigh. When she's not at work, she is usually with her husband and two children. She sets goals for her family and work life. She appreciates her organization's family care plans, family-friendly work events, and work-from-home incentives.

Boomer profile: Chris has spent twenty years in the IT/software workspace. He doesn't have kids and spends his downtime exploring far-off countries with his friends. He writes a blog about protecting minorities' rights. He loves his organization's flexible working options and the ability to work when traveling.

How well did your stereotypes match up with the actual profiles?

START-STOP-CONTINUE EXERCISE

Ask yourself these start-stop-continue questions:

Start—*What am I not doing that I need to* start *doing, to reduce my use of Illicit Transference and curb it within my team?*

Stop—*What am I currently doing that I need to* stop *doing, to reduce my use of Illicit Transference and curb it within my team?*

Continue—*What am I currently doing that I should* continue *doing, to reduce my use of Illicit Transference and curb it within my team?*

I hope you will now catch yourself in the act of Illicit Transference before you let assumptions get the better of you. Something as simple as giving people the benefit of doubt will make you a better human. And by the way, we Brits don't all like fish and chips either!

Carrying on the British theme, we'll start the next chapter with something we all subconsciously do that can inhibit our ability to truly connect with people.

CHAPTER 11

RELATIONSHIP BIAS #2
SIMILAR TO ME

If you are a woman and you walk into a room full of men and one other woman, you will likely gravitate to the other woman. Same thing if you're a man entering a room full of women. Age, ethnicity, dress, and profession are other surface traits that draw us together. We automatically feel a degree of comfort with people we share something in common with.

We feel an even greater level of comfort with people who share our point of view and interests. That's why we form clubs and gravitate to online communities. Not a problem, as long as we're aware of it. It's when we're not aware of it that it can limit us—and the Relationships we form.

With the Similar to Me cognitive bias, humans tend to get along with other humans who look, act, and think like they do. Though there may be situations where "opposites attract," similarity is a far more prevalent factor in determining our initial attraction to other people, as numerous studies have shown.[1]

Other names for this bias might be trait narcissism, "caught up in your own reflection," and affinity bias. No matter what we call it and no matter what our background is, we all tend to like people who have similar characteristics to us. This is because the brain is naturally discriminatory, and that can be a problem—especially in work settings. This bias interferes with our ability to create deep-level diversity in our teams. For example, if we expect everyone to think and process things the same way we do, then yes, our team will be easier to manage, but we'll also greatly limit the assortment of personalities, strengths, cultures, and ideas we can draw from.

Similar to Me

In America, whenever I hear a British person say, "Oh, you're British, right?" we strike up a conversation. We laugh, we smile, maybe we even swap phone numbers and agree to meet again. Our commonality, shallow as it may be, draws us together. This is a simple example of the Similar to Me Bias.

The bias: We are naturally drawn to people who look, act, and think like us.

The effect on Relationships: We act favorably toward some people and unfavorably toward others, based on their similarity to us.

The cure: *Stop* surrounding yourself with people like you. *Start* challenging yourself to engage with all types of people from all walks of life.

Rewarding People Like Us

Leaders exhibit the Similar to Me Bias when they encourage their teams to behave like them and unwittingly reward people for such behaviors. That's exactly how this bias tripped me up.

Rightly or wrongly, the only lifestyle I know is to work hard. It was something my Mum instilled into me as far back as I can remember. I've always felt I needed to strive; otherwise, I wouldn't have money to do the things I wanted. I am a worker bee. I am drawn to other worker bees. I feel an immediate sense of connection with anyone who goes above and beyond the call of duty to get sh*t done.

In the early years of my career, I embraced hard work at the expense of personal time. I was drawn to those people on my team who also worked seven days a week. I would regularly send weekend emails, evening emails, and early morning emails. And when people responded to these, I felt rewarded. I got a dopamine fix. In turn, I would send even more off-hour emails.

I cringe now to think of the emotional damage I caused my team with my weekend, early morning, and late-night missives. Not to mention the unfairness of my expectations—I was the founder/owner of the company; to ask hired people to work just as hard as I did was unreasonable. But my brain assumed that if folks weren't working 24/7, they were lazy and not passionate about our cause. The ones who worked harder received more of my time and attention, and I forged stronger bonds with them. It was hard for me to form connections with people who were not like me.

In job interviews for new hires, I asked questions like, "Did you work hard throughout university?" and "Are you a strict forty-hour-week person?" And if they gave answers that differed from my own . . .

NEXT! I wanted to hire clones of myself. Mini-me's. I can't think of anything worse!

Even in my group of friends and in rugby practice, I was drawn to people who seemed to put in more work than others. Whether they actually *contributed* more or not was a different story. Ultimately, my bias didn't help my business. As part of my busy-bee persona, I am also an "activator" type. I like to push the start button and figure things out on the fly. But because I surrounded myself with other activator types, my team would often start working on a project even when there wasn't a clear path or outcome in mind. We ended up with a culture of *ready, shoot, aim.*

How many good people did I fail to hire due to the Similar to Me Bias? How many good people did I lose because of this?

Making the shift

After losing most of my employees, it became apparent that we needed to create a better culture than the one we had. *My* values were not necessarily shared by everyone else on the team. Nor should they be, I realized. So, we began to create a new culture at DX with new values—a main area of focus being the value of working smart over working hard. We talk about it a lot.

My shift in understanding productivity has helped me recognize that it's not about working twelve to fourteen hours a day; it's about working efficiently so that you get the output you need within a reasonable time frame. Working fewer hours is still only an aspirational goal for *me*, alas, but my shift in thinking has allowed me to stop my brain from calling people lazy if they refuse to sacrifice their personal time for work. It has helped me connect better with others and hire people who are not like me. I can't think of anything worse than a hundred Alexes at DX. All we'd talk about is soccer, prawn cocktail crisps, and *Ted Lasso*! And we'd be missing out on all those added strengths that diverse teammates bring to the table.

I have hired a team who are not like me and don't think like me on purpose. My hardworking nature has been balanced out with people who are more efficient and smart-working. While I may not have a "best buddy" at work who sees everything the way I do, I have a team of people who bring varying perspectives to the table. This enables me to learn something new every day and empowers us to achieve more together. We have strong Relationships that are formed from curiosity and respect for each other. We meet others where they are, without judgment. What may be a little weird for me works wonders for them. In our differences, we thrive.

If you want to accomplish the same thing, I recommend thinking in terms of culture *add* versus culture *fit*. Hire and surround yourself with people who *add* to the culture with their unique perspectives rather than just hiring

> Think(ing) in terms of culture *add* versus culture *fit*.

people who fit in with the *current* culture. That way, you shake up stale thinking and gain exposure to new, more often than not better, ideas and approaches.

More than the sum of parts

If you hire the same profiles across your team, you create a lot of redundancy, and you get diminishing returns on new hires. Good, CAREing leaders want teams that are "more than the sum of their parts." By diversifying, your team can accomplish more together than they would on their own. People's strengths compensate for one another's deficits, and you create more well-rounded competencies overall. And you can't do that when you surround yourself with *you*-clones.

This principle applies to nonwork relationships as well. I married Karoline, a woman who's the complete opposite of me. Being vulnerable and allowing myself to form close bonds with someone who thinks and acts so differently from me has been a test of my ability to conquer the Similar to Me Bias. It has also given me the best relationship I've ever had. Neither of us is ever bored with the other. Every day I gain perspectives and insights I wouldn't have gained in a carbon-copy marriage. The experiences and debates that ensue from having relationships with someone dissimilar to you will push you to do things outside your comfort zone, which activates your growth mindset.

> The more we expose ourselves to new ideas and perspectives, the greater number of cognitive doors we open.

The more we expose ourselves to new ideas and perspectives, the greater number of cognitive doors we open. We see things in new ways. We are more likely to try new things. As we continue to do this, and are rewarded for it, the brain begins to relax its Similar to Me Bias and new possibilities can arise in our lives more often.

A Similar to Me Bias in families

A friend of mine told me about how her father was athletic and sports-minded, which led to relationship problems with his firstborn son, whom we'll call Craig.

Craig, it seems, was born without an athletic bone in his body. The father tried to force baseball and numerous other sports on him to no avail. The more the father forced the sports issue with Craig, the more frustrated they both became, to the point of tears and exhaustion. The problem was exacerbated by the fact that the second son in the family was a natural athlete. The father was pushing Craig away while favoring (even if unintentionally) the son he could take out on the ball field or golf course.

How the dad ended up solving this bias—before totally screwing Craig up—was by finding something Craig was interested in and taking up that hobby with him. This happened to be theater—not something Dad had ever tried. But he figured he could at least show up at the community theater and help with set design since he loved architecture and art. It just so happened that the play had a part for an older gentleman, and Dad agreed to do it. Father and son both ended up on stage and loving it! They found an interest they could share, which gave them a way to spend time together in a meaningful way. Craig no longer felt like the odd man out. And Dad's new hobby kindled a love for theater that trickled down to his other children, including his daughter (my friend), who is now pursuing a career in the film industry.

In a very real sense, my friend owes her career choice to the breaking of a bias. A nice fringe benefit that continues to bear fruit today.

Kick This Bias to the Curb

The Similar to Me Bias must be taken seriously and weeded out. Not only does it create limitations in our thinking, but it can lead to ethical, moral, and social problems in the workplace. Leaders who are gripped by this bias tend—often unknowingly—to use unfair practices in the hiring and treatment of staff. When interviewing new hires, they look for people who resemble themselves. The bias even kicks in when evaluating and promoting existing staff. Research has shown that when superiors formally evaluate their subordinates, "The more similar the parties are, the higher rating the superior tends to give. This tendency applies with respect to several different dimensions of similarity, such as similarity of values and habits, similarity of beliefs about the way things should be at work, and similarity with respect to demographic variables (such as age, race, gender, and work experience)."[2]

This bias can occur in the other direction as well. Subordinates tend to be more trusting and confident in supervisors whom they perceive to be similar to themselves. Consequently, they may have more of a positive relationship with such individuals, and this may lead their superiors, in turn, to judge them more favorably. Thus, the relationship, driven by the bias, becomes self-perpetuating in deeply rooted ways.

If unchecked, this bias can cause us to ignore, leave out, judge, or grant less privilege to those we perceive as unlike us. It can also lead to unethical, and even illegal, discrimination in hiring. Of course, hiring is discriminatory by nature. Aside from the fact that AI does not CARE, and most people don't even make it to the interview process since unfair résumé-profiling bots leave personality fit out of the equation, the interviewers are still human. As you have learned, humans have brains and brains have thousands of heuristics that lead to biases, which you might not even know are making false, negative assumptions about the people being interviewed. You are trying to differentiate among candidates and choose the best fit. The problem is that many of us aren't aware of when and how our discrimination veers into the unfair, unethical, and even illegal range.

Most of us know outright discrimination is wrong. For example, if we are white, we won't refuse to hire someone because they are black. But we may devalue the education they received from a historically black college, such as Spelman College or Howard University, when compared to other candidates who went to universities that we are more familiar with and consider more prestigious, like Harvard or Yale. Or we may favor a candidate who grew up locally and who has local experiences we recognize rather than someone whose education/experience occurred abroad in a place or institution we're unfamiliar with.

We have a responsibility to become aware of this bias and do everything we can to fight it. This might require training, coaching, consultation, and other proactive means of opening our eyes, but it most definitely requires seeking continual feedback from our teams. Biases, by their nature, are blind spots. As leaders, we need to be brave enough to constantly ask our staff if we are making fair and unbiased decisions. This can happen only in a psychologically safe environment. We also need to involve people who are demographically unlike ourselves in hiring, firing, and promotion decisions. This can help us compensate for unconscious biases and can help diverse candidates feel more comfortable during the interview processes.

Social Bubble Blindness

Rooting out the Similar to Me Bias on a *superficial* level (e.g., by hiring people from different demographic groups) is only part of the solution. Remember, the brain is a connection machine. It is *programmed* to look for commonalities. This means that even if you're self-aware, open-minded, and inclined to accept diversity, you may still have to fight against the hardwiring of your brain which dutifully seeks similarity.

There is a part of the brain known as the *reticular activating system* (RAC) which regulates arousal. Not sexual arousal but rather the brain's ability to wake up and pay attention. The RAC tells us what to act on and pay attention to by filtering *out* unimportant details and filtering *in* those elements we deem significant. Have you ever bought a new car and suddenly every other driver on the road seems to be driving that same car? When I had a VW Beetle, my brain saw Beetles everywhere. That's the RAC at work. Do you ever smile at another driver as if you're instant friends because you drive the same car? There is an instant sense of comradery. The brain seeks out an "arousal" experience by looking for traits that connect us to other people—similar interests, values, tastes, politics, jobs, family situations, and so on. It's important to realize that the brain is *designed* to look for sameness, and it feels rewarded and comforted when it finds it. We must be aware of the immense power of this natural tendency.

Though we may regard our social and professional circles as marvelously diverse, we may be ignoring underlying similarities. My friend group, for example, contains both men and women, multiple races and ethnicities, a range of ages, and the whole sexuality spectrum, but underneath these differences lies the fact that these people are mostly in the same field I'm in or have similar personality traits.

This underscores the need to differentiate between surface-level diversity and deep-level diversity. You don't achieve deep diversity simply by making your team look like an ethnically diverse college brochure. The key to *true* diversity on your team is not to focus on demographics or superficialities but rather to look for people who approach the world from divergent intellectual and emotional angles—angles that will help you solve problems innovatively and develop products and services that address a wider range of humanity.

Hire people who have different working styles from you. Different personalities. Different approaches. This allows you to consider solutions from multiple directions. It also allows you to offset your own tendencies. If you like to make decisions at warp speed, for example, it may benefit you to partner with someone who slows down the decision-making process and carefully weighs each factor. The two of you will balance each other out.

Overcoming the Bias

Here's how I approach the Similar to Me Bias. I remind myself that, whomever I am dealing with, we are all unique in fascinating and valuable ways, but at the end of the day, we have vastly more in common than whatever separates us. We all yearn for connection, meaning, and security in our lives. We all have loved ones we care about. We all want to do better for ourselves and our families. And we all share many of the same cognitive biases; otherwise, this book wouldn't make sense to anyone but me. Because we share such profound commonalities deep down, there is no "threat" in befriending someone who is different from us in cultural and intellectual ways; there is only the promise of learning more about who we all are as connected human beings.

If you want a well-rounded team that can attack and solve problems from all angles, it can't be made up of clones. You need people who *break* the pattern—people who bring *different* skills, talents, ideas, and personalities to the table. I have a low preference for Clarity; I don't need that much in order for my brain to feel safe. That means when it comes to strategy, it's in my head and I am pretty comfortable not having one. So, I make sure I have people that surround me who have a high preference for Clarity and can help me formulate strategy and communicate that effectively. Or maybe you have a lot of technical, detail-oriented thinkers on your team, which are great to have, and you balance that out by hiring people who are big-picture idea people, which brings some fresh creativity to the workplace. I made sure we have a diverse team when it comes to what we do outside of work. A team of soccer fans (like me) would get pretty boring! We have people who like to bake, go to the gym, play golf, see plays, and have varying tastes in extracurricular activities. Balancing the strengths and interests of your team is where higher performance comes from.

Nothing is more exciting, in fact, than to have a group of wildly different personalities and backgrounds working in unity towards a common goal. Of course, this introduces challenges as well. Healthy debate and conflict can emerge from bringing different types together, but a skilled leader knows how to manage conflict and turn that friction into productive outcomes.

We are the sum of our experiences and relationships. The more types of people we can interact with, the more "complete" we become as human beings. The more complete we are (we never get there, but we try), the better leaders we can be to the widest range of people.

> We are the sum of our experiences and relationships.

Often, when we connect with new people, we look for commonalities and ignore the differences because those can be harder to navigate. Sameness-seeking may be easier for initial conversations, but it doesn't necessarily lead to the breaking of new ground nor does it make for well-rounded relationships or teams.

To break out of the sameness bubble, you need to shake your workplace up as well as your own network. Invite team members who are very unlike you—mentally, culturally, and emotionally—to participate in the interviewing and hiring process, to help ensure you're not hiring *you*-clones. Work with a consultant to analyze your team's personality types or working styles, and try to pair people up in complementary and interesting ways. Get people to see the world from a different perspective. On LinkedIn, purposely look to connect with people who are not like you and whom you could learn from.

As leaders, we want to develop the emotional intelligence to recognize that, despite people's differences, everyone yearns for the same things, such as Clarity, Autonomy and Relationships—they just seek it in different ways and at different levels. This allows us to live by the mantra: "Treat people how *they* want to be treated" (not how *we* want to treat them). That's known as Equity, and it's what we will explore in the final piece of the CARE Equation.

Let's Work It

You're hiring, and it's down to two candidates.

Candidate A is quite different from you in age, gender, ethnicity, and background. But the two of you converse easily and you discover,

159

to your mutual surprise, that you have several common interests. You find the candidate super likeable, and you laugh out loud several times during the interview. Maybe you discover that you have several of the same favorite Netflix shows. They answer a test question in a way that instantly resonates with you. You are eager to have a more diverse team, so this potential hire intrigues and excites you. However, their degree and experience don't *exactly* suit the role you have available. They seem coachable and trainable though.

Candidate B is similar to you in age, gender, and background but is a bit less in sync with you. The interview isn't as fun as the one with Candidate A, but you respect the candidate's intelligence and skill. You disagree on the right answer to one of your interview questions, but they offer a very interesting perspective, and it gets you thinking that you might want to update that question. Their demographic similarity to you makes you reluctant to hire them, from a diversity perspective, and the lack of a "spark" between you is another strike against this hire.

However, they have excellent references and an even better skill set—one that matches well with the needs of your team. Who would you hire in this scenario? Answer honestly. Why? What are some of the benefits of deep-level diversity on your team? What are some of the consequences of having a team that is too mentally homogenous? This is the challenge we face in hiring. We don't always have the luxury of time on our side in order to build the trust and Relationships with people to understand what really makes them tick and to know who is the right fit.

In the above case, it's a tough choice. Circumstances might lead you to choose one or the other. Candidate A could be great if you have a well-established team where there is lots of Clarity and Autonomy. Their coachability and divergent background might add some creativity to existing systems and processes that are well tested. Candidate B might be great if it's a new team without much Clarity and therefore not much Autonomy. You need someone who has experience and expertise who can help form the structure needed. No spark required.

So, the short answer is, it depends. It depends on the circumstances. It depends on the unique individual(s) in question. We need to tailor our approach to the situation. There is no one-size-fits-all approach. That's the power and importance of Equity.

START-STOP-CONTINUE EXERCISE

Ask yourself these start-stop-continue questions:

Start—*What am I not doing that I need to* start *doing, to change the Similar to Me Bias in myself and my team?*

Stop—*What am I currently doing that I need to* stop *doing, to change the Similar to Me Bias in myself and my team?*

Continue—*What am I currently doing that I should* continue *doing, to change the Similar to Me Bias in myself and my team?*

ON RELATIONSHIPS

The "R" factor (Relationships) is the most important part of the CARE Equation. Organizations and teams are nothing but bunches of humans. Every human is uniquely different. We all yearn to have trusting connections with our peers, with the people we work for, and with the people who work for us.

Relationships are all about going below the surface and getting to know each and every person you serve as the full human beings they are. That means deliberately and intentionally spending quality time with your team to talk about nonwork stuff and *do* nonwork stuff. It also means developing vulnerability and curiosity. The more open and curious you are—the more you ask and listen—the deeper the connections you will forge and the more trust you will gain.

Don't let the Illicit Transference and Similar to Me biases prevent you from getting to know all the people on your team and from hiring the best and brightest individuals. These biases are dangerous brain tendencies that must be actively overcome.

Relationships build the human trust needed for psychological safety to flourish. You must get past assumptions to see the real person. It's not about being best friends with everybody or having a "family" at work. It's just about knowing the people you work with at the basic human level. It takes time and energy to get to know humans, but it's well worth the effort when the guardrails go down and we stop questioning the other person's motives and gossiping about what we assume of others. Our brains will thank us, too, when they feel cognitively safe enough to speak up and be authentic.

To know is not to assume. Having open and honest conversations is where we truly build mutual trust and respect. If one of my team members is burnt out, I need to know; I don't have a crystal ball. My team telling me what motivates them, how they are feeling, and what is going on in their lives allows me to better connect and anticipate their needs. However, if you do all the talking and you don't use those gifts of two ears and one mouth in that ratio, they will be silent and their guards will go up. And it's hard to build a high-performing team when the guards are up.

Signs that your team members feel safe:
- They openly collaborate.
- They check in with each other throughout the day.
- They continually ask questions and show curiosity toward each other.
- They ask you questions about who you are as their leader.

Signs that your team members do not feel safe:
- They isolate.
- They don't connect with one another.
- Their heads are always down.
- You hear them gossiping and making wrong assumptions about others.

Which of the above sets of characteristics best describes your team?

SAFE

UNSAFE

To review:

CLARITY is the WHAT

AUTONOMY is the HOW

RELATIONSHIPS are the WHO

Clarity is about making sure people are on the same line of the same page and not in different books. It means working hard to reduce communication assumptions and to clarify expectations and goals. It means asking great questions to make sure everyone is aligned.

Autonomy is about giving people a say in how things are done and making them feel a sense of freedom and ownership within clearly defined parameters. It means giving as much control as the situation allows you to versus being in control.

Relationships ensure that people feel a sense of belonging, inclusion, and connection. To achieve the "R" part of the CARE equation, leaders must really know each of the humans they serve—their motivations, the experiences they've been through, and the challenges they are going through now. It's the *"Who"* to the *"What"* and the *"How"*. After all, "R is the human part of the equation, and how can you treat people the way they want and need to be treated if you don't know them? Remember, humans—both workers and leaders—cannot be replaced by AI. It doesn't CARE and never will. Humans do. This is how we differentiate ourselves in the technology revolution and why working effectively with other people will help us win.

The next part, "E" (Equity), ties all the components of the CARE Equation together.

PART IV

CARE

Clarity

Autonomy

Relationships

Equity

CHAPTER 12

THE IMPORTANCE OF
EQUITY

Clarity, Autonomy, and Relationships are the foundational ingredients for building high-performance teams. The final component of the CARE equation is "E"—Equity—and it's what pulls the WHAT (Clarity), the HOW (Autonomy), and the WHO (Relationships) together. Equity sustains a high-performing culture over time and is achieved by tailoring your approach to the unique needs of each individual in order to pull out their best performance possible. It ensures that every team member feels a sense of fairness and a sense of being met *where they're at*. This is where true psychological safety comes from. Equity is the gauge for higher performance and how you really win.

Defining Equity

Equal is not equitable. I remember a time when everyone on my team received a thirty-minute check-in meeting with me every week. Seemed to make sense, right? I wanted to ensure everyone had equal amounts of my time, energy, and resources. But when I took a closer look, this idea wasn't working out so well. The thirty-minute allotment, although "equal" for all, was completely arbitrary. Some people needed no time from me, some needed five minutes, and some needed an hour or more. The people who thought of this as too much time from me were thinking, "Doesn't he trust me to do my job?" or "What a waste of time." The people who felt it was too little time were thinking, "Aren't I important enough to merit more of his attention?" Either way, my failure to deliver Equity was triggering the threat circuitry in their brains.

Many people think Equity means equality. The words are similar, so they're easily confused. Equality means dividing up the pie into same-size portions and giving everyone an equal piece. But that does not amount to fairness or usefulness because people's needs are different. Equity means slicing the pie slice according to the needs and wants of each individual.

Look at the illustration at the start of the chapter. In an Equality scenario, you would give each person a ladder of the same size, perhaps one of medium height. This would be *equal* treatment, but it wouldn't be helpful to either party—the person on the right requires only a short stepstool; the person on the left requires a tall ladder. The illustration, as drawn, demonstrates Equity. Each person has what they need to do the job effectively.

Our definition of Equity, therefore, is *providing the right amount of resources and attention to people on the basis of their needs.* This also means giving people resources and attention in the *way* they need and want it. Not everyone responds the same way to the same approach.

> Equity . . . is providing the right amount of resources and attention to people on the basis of their needs.

A member of my DX team, Abigail, craves certainty. Without the certainty she needs, she gets a little bit upset. Her role in business operations depends on Clarity. She thrives on having expectations clearly outlined. She's not right, and she's not wrong; certainty is just what her brain needs to be at cognitive ease. I am the opposite. For my brain to be at cognitive ease, I don't need as much Clarity. I can thrive in ambiguity. I am not right or wrong. However, my job as a leader is to know Abigail and treat her how *she* wants to be treated and not how I want to be treated. That means giving her the Clarity she craves to be successful and not the amount I crave. It's all about preferences and ensuring the preferences of our *teams* are met—not our own. That's overcoming our biases and assumptions, adapting to their needs, and being inclusive. In this scenario with Abigail, I'll ask her more questions than I ask others because I understand that when she has enough Clarity, her brain is at cognitive ease, and she is better able to perform her job. I give her more than I am comfortable because that is the right thing to do.

Equity, History, and the Brain

As *Homo sapiens*, we have a long-standing desire to receive an adequate allocation of the resources of our tribe. When we perceive that allocation to be unfair, our insula is activated.[1] The insula is a part of the brain involved in processing subjective experiences and making judgements about them. Feelings of disgust are believed to originate

Unfairness disgusts and demotivates us.

in the insula.[2] When we perceive unfairness—toward ourselves and even toward others—we become disgusted. Unfairness disgusts and demotivates us. However, the insula is also tied to motivation.[3] We are motivated to pursue situations that produce feelings of joy and to avoid situations that produce negative feelings.

In simple situations, when no context is provided, equality is often used as a measure of fairness. None of us want to receive a smaller benefit than the next person. However, when we understand more about the *context* of the distribution, our sense of fairness changes. Equity kicks in. That conference ticket we were hoping to use . . . maybe the new hire would benefit more from it than we would.

Homo sapiens learned the concept of Equity early on. Fifteen thousand years ago, distributing food *equally* throughout the tribe would not have worked. It would have underserved those who needed more food than others, such as pregnant women, hunters, or those who had to go on long journeys to find water. When you went out on hunting duties, you needed more nutrition than others because you expended more calories. One banana each would not have been fair for all.

An *equitable* distribution of food thus became the norm. It was to everyone's benefit to have the hunters well-fueled for their arduous tasks and journeys. Therefore, other tribe members were happy to give their berries to the hunters, even if it meant perhaps enduring some short-term hunger themselves. They knew that if the hunters came back with meat, it could mean abundance for everyone and that they were all more likely to survive—for them, winning. Similarly, if there was an ill person in the tribe, another tribe member might give up their fur to keep them warm, knowing that the sooner the sick person recovered, the sooner they could begin contributing to the tribe again. Giving resources to the sick also ensured the tribe's numbers would remain strong and would increase their chances of survival.

Equity requires higher-level thinking instead of our default knee-jerk selfishness. It demands a big-picture perspective. We recognize that we may need to receive less of some resources in general or at the moment but that this will benefit our own good in the end. When the whole tribe thrives, we thrive along with it. A bigger pot of caribou stew ultimately means bigger servings for everyone.

Equity also means that *we* receive more of the resources that are most important to *our* role and *our* particular way of thriving. When distribution is equitable, no one is really suffering.

The concept of fair and equitable distribution of resources, though developed thousands of years ago for survival, carries into the modern workplace. The same rules still apply. Equity means proportionately providing resources and attention to those that need it and in the amounts they need it, knowing that what is good for the team is ultimately good for all individuals who make up the team. It means giving everyone more of the resources they, in particular, require and less of the resources they don't. This is a big part of leadership—ensuring that time, energy, and attention are allocated where they are needed most and where they can do the most good for each individual and for the entire team. Put simply, it's adaptation and intentionality—it's the hard work in doing what is right versus what is easy.

Fairness Matters

A Pew Research study indicates that perceptions of being treated unfairly are a major reason people quit their jobs.[4] Concomitantly, according to a survey of 3,500 employees conducted by the *Harvard Business Review*, "Perceptions of a more fair [sic] employee experience improves employee performance by up to 26 percent and employee retention by up to 27 percent."[5] This perception of fairness, interestingly enough, does not derive largely from improved hiring and promotion policies but rather from employees' day-to-day experience of fairness in the workplace.[6] Leaders play a huge role in providing this daily sense of fairness.

Everyone wants to be treated fairly. Everyone. Regardless of gender, race, nationality, or age. Even children, from the moment they realize what Equity is, will shout, "It's not fair!" when they perceive inequity. Providing Equity is a huge part of the job of leadership.

Going back to my example of the forced thirty-minute meeting every week, both those who needed more of my time and those who needed less had a negative reaction to this "equal shares for all" approach. However, when I'm more intentional with my distribution of time and resources, people feel a sense that they're getting what *they* want and not what I arbitrarily decide they should get—thus lowering the probability that anyone feels unfairly treated or doesn't get what they need.

> ### Good leaders manage their time well.

Good leaders manage their time well, making deliberate time and space for one-on-one check-ins with staff. Some people need five minutes and some people need an hour, but a good leader is available for whatever time is needed. If I had known what I know now about Equity, I would have saved myself a lot of time (quite literally) during those check-ins. I would have also saved my people from a lot of unnecessary stress because I would have adapted and evolved my behavior and actions to match how *they* need to be treated. Making time for employees pays itself forward in the type of environment it creates. Getting Equity right will end up making time your friend, not your enemy, and allow you to distribute the finite amount of time you are given to where it is needed the most.

Once you have this locked down, conversations during those meetings can flow easier. Asking questions about their life and their time builds those deep connections that are essential to ensuring Equity. Begin with some version of, "What's going on in your world?" Making the effort to discover what's happening in the personal lives of team members leads to deeper connections. Like with my team, if I didn't know what was going on in my people's lives or what made them tick, how on earth would I have been able to create an environment that services them, which later helps the whole team win? Questions also helps the leader understand who might need special considerations at the present time.

Bottom line: If you don't make time for your employees and connect with them, you cannot create an environment that's equitable. Making time and asking questions, being open to feedback and change, and checking our assumptions at the door so biases aren't kicking in will bring us to these better relationships that will create more Equity in our employees' day-to-day lives. And when you do these things consistently over time, people gain a sense of, "My boss is trying hard to be fair and treat me how I want to be treated!"

As social creatures, we have a natural sense of fairness, and when we receive too little of a resource, our sense of disgust is triggered. But this sense can also be triggered when we receive too much. Imagine if you were given a huge corner office (way more space than you needed), but the production team in the adjacent room was crowded into a tiny area, barely able to function. You would naturally feel uncomfortable and would want to give some of your space to the people making the products.

A new trainee generally needs more of a boss's attention than a twenty-year veteran does. And no one perceives unfairness when the boss gives that new person more time and energy. A team member who takes on added responsibilities receives higher pay and gets greater access to office equipment and support staff. This, too, is viewed as inherently fair. More responsibility means more benefits. However, when someone gets higher pay and greater access to resources without bringing any added value to the team, this is seen as inherently unfair.

Unfairness triggers disgust. And disgust regarding your job leads to anger, burnout, and stress. How can a one-size-fits-all leadership style be fair when every human is different and has unique needs?

"E" Goes Back to "R"

Taking the time to build strong Relationships with every team member is essential. That's how you find out who each person is and what their needs are. And that's how you determine how much time, energy, and resources that person needs. You can't know those things unless you know the *person*. You can't do "E" without "R."

In turn, what sustains Relationships is to provide everyone with equitable treatment. You do this by knowing where the team is at and who needs more time and attention today, this week, and this month. Equity ensures that the leader's Relationships with the team remain mutually beneficial over time and are based on data, not assumptions.

The key, again, is to give everyone on the team what *they* need, not what *you* need. This is not easy or natural, and it requires enormous commitment and dedication on the part of a leader. You must set your naturally selfish orientation aside and try to see things from others' perspectives, which you can only do by building Relationships.

If I were to treat everyone as I would like to be treated in a business context, everyone would be fully autonomous and self-empowered. I'd assume everyone was comfortable talking openly on all topics. And because I work unhealthily hard, with too few resources and rewards (as many entrepreneurs do), I'd expect my team to happily burn both ends of the candle together.

This would be hell for some people. It would also be an unreasonable ask on my part—expecting people to work just as hard as the company owner when they don't have as much to gain or lose. The only way it wouldn't be hell is if I hired a team of people who were all just like me—which is a mistake many leaders make. If we surround ourselves with people exactly like us, we miss out on having a diverse team. We build a culture based on a shared set of traits rather than a dynamic variety of traits.

Imagine being hired into an Alex culture that thrives on experimentation and open-endedness when your mind craves Clarity. Your brain enjoys working within boundaries, while Alex and the rest of the team love being fiercely independent with few parameters. You would not be getting what you needed at work, you'd feel utterly isolated, and you would go home every day with the foul taste of unfairness in your mouth.

In a culture of Equity, on the other hand, the employee who craves defined expectations gets the level of Clarity they need to feel safe. The employee who wants only a small bit of guidance and a few guardrails gets enough Autonomy to excite them. And the employee who doesn't feel comfortable sharing every detail in their life is allowed to have some privacy and knows they don't have to bare their soul to feel a sense of Relationship.

Three Key Behaviors

One of the chief skills a leader needs is the ability to "read a room." Your job is to respond, in real time, to the dynamically changing needs of your team, not force people to slot themselves into the neat little management boxes you have set up to make yourself feel in control. In working from an Equity perspective, you can read a room easier and reinforce Equity when adhering to three important behaviors:

1. **Be flexible and responsive.** Life happens, and sometimes employees have personal issues that may prevent them from dedicating all their time and energy to work. As a leader, do your part to lighten their load. Of course, this is a delicate balance because there are still employment expectations to be met, but try to adjust workloads and deadlines. Take away some stress and add a bit of support. Maybe give them a day or two off—especially if they have given extra hours to the company when asked.

2. **Distribute resources dynamically.** When a person joins your team, especially if they are new to the company and culture, they will need more guidance and attention than the rest of your team. And from time to time, certain members of your team may be pulling heavier workloads than everyone else. Perhaps they're on a time-sensitive project for a high-profile client. Look out for these scenarios and give them more resources when they need them.

3. **Consistently deliver what you promised.** Humans crave predictability, and we want to know that our behaviors lead to expected outcomes. If we perform well, we want to be recognized. If our performance suffers, we should expect to receive constructive feedback with suggestions for improvement. As a leader, it's your job to deliver this consistency, even as you strive to tailor your attention to individual needs. That means rewarding everyone in a consistent way and not playing favorites. Not everyone needs to be rewarded in the same *manner*, but everyone needs to be rewarded and critiqued equitably and consistently.

START-STOP-CONTINUE EXERCISE

Before we move on, ask yourself these start-stop-continue questions:

Start—*What am I not doing that I need to* start *doing, to create more Equity in my team?*

Stop—*What am I currently doing that I need to* stop *doing, to create more Equity in my team?*

Continue—*What am I currently doing that I should* continue *doing, to create more Equity in my team?*

To achieve Equity in a team is to multiply the success of every other component of the CARE Equation. Equity leads to fairness. Fairness leads to psychological safety. Psychological safety leads to a culture where everyone on the team has a voice and uses it. Those voices, when harnessed, lead to higher-performing teams.

Now let's look at a couple of common biases that put a damper on Equity.

CHAPTER 13

EQUITY BIAS #1
DEFAULT EFFECT

Every human is different. Treating each member on your team the same way isn't fair. I learned the hard way that the same thirty-minute check-in meeting with each direct report—using the same agenda and meeting template—does not work. How can the same allotment of time, with the same questions asked each week, work for every person? It doesn't!

My mistake was in making the *default choice* I had observed other managers making. A default choice often seems like a no-brainer. And it *is*. But a brain is actually required when you're leading a team.

The Default Effect

In my busy—sometimes overly busy—work life, defaulting to the seemingly easiest decision is a habit that often comes back to bite me. I remember deciding I wanted to improve scheduling coordination amongst my team members. So I said to everyone, without giving it much thought, "I expect you all to use your calendar exactly the same way I do, so we can see what each other is doing and we can coordinate more easily." Seemed like an easy and sensible choice. The kind of thing a boss does all the time.

Well, it came down like a ton of bricks. Some had their own calendars that worked better for them and ones that they'd been using for years. Others used Microsoft Calendar in a totally different way. What seemed like a great decision for the group was not perceived as fair and equitable for everyone. After some thought and discussion, we found a simple and effective way to coordinate our daily schedules that worked well for everyone, including me.

Welcome to the Default Effect—the tendency to pick the default choice rather than looking for contextual details when making decisions. The chooser makes an easy, passive choice as opposed to an active, fully considered one. Their lazy brain gets the better of them. Assumptions strike again!

The bias: When presented with a choice, we tend to pick the default option without thoroughly examining the context and implications.

The effect on Equity: We assume our decision makes sense for everyone, even when it doesn't. And we treat people inequitably as a result.

The cure: *Stop* automatically choosing the easiest path. *Start* ensuring that you have considered all the options—and the context—before diving into action.

How the Default Effect Works

There are two ways this bias works:

Endogenous Default Effect: By failing to make an active choice, you end up with whatever the default option is. An example would be going with whatever health insurance plan is presented to you without reviewing alternative plans or customizing the payment options.

Exogenous Default Effect: Choosing the default implied by the situation or by social trend. "I did it because everyone else was doing it!" An example would be choosing one product over another just because you have seen others using it.

People are likely to make the same decisions they observe others making, and it derives from a survival behavior where we learned by copying other humans: "Monkey see, monkey do." If we don't know enough about a situation, we emulate someone else, even if we have no reason to believe they know more than we do. To the human mind, a choice that's already been made by someone else is safer than a random chance, even if it lacks personal context or reasoning.

Another way to explain this is that the brain defaults to the choice that requires the least effort. Making decisions consumes a lot of brain power. Rather than expend precious energy, people often go with the premade or

> The brain defaults to the choice that requires the least effort.

seemingly obvious choice. Choosing an *equal* distribution of resources, rather than an *equitable* distribution, is a classic example of the Default Effect. You have a metaphorical pie, so you divide it equally amongst everyone in the group, regardless of whether everyone needs or even *wants* pie—because that seems, by default, to be "fair." It's definitely a lot easier than taking the time to consider everyone's individual needs. So if someone doesn't like pie, so to speak, they get it anyway—too bad. This can trigger feelings of unfairness that lead to disgust.

When I was giving equal one-on-one times rather than equitable one-on-ones for my DX staff, I started to get a little peeved at the group that didn't seem to benefit as much from the designated half-hour time. My brain assumed they were not interested and didn't care. I later learned that many of them, in fact, were thinking, *"I just want to talk with Alex as needed; why do we need to use this stupid thirty-minute template?"* Some liked the structure as it was, some needed more time from me than the allotted thirty minutes, and some needed less. I began to see that a one-size-fits-all strategy does not work, and neither does relying on the status quo.

It is easier to distribute things equally. It feels safer too. *If everyone gets the same amount, no one will be offended.* The opposite ends up happening though. People receive what *you decide* they require rather than what they actually require and then they end up offended anyway.

Leadership is all about setting people up to do their best work and be their best selves. As a team member, when you are treated inequitably, you don't feel seen, and this leads to stress and lower engagement levels. Going home from work with that feeling of unfairness every night has a detrimental effect on both your work life and your nonwork life.

After realizing the error of my ways, I switched to a more equitable and fair approach. I now have monthly "check-ins" with no time limit or minimum and no one-size-fits-all template. I just ask folks, "What's on your mind right now that would be useful for us to talk about? What's something you need from me that will empower you to be successful? What is motivating you right now?" My goal is to move to weekly check-ins—*if* they're needed. I am already hearing people say they enjoy that time and get a lot out of the meeting. And if people don't want to talk, that's okay too!

On Mondays I keep my lunchtime schedule free for anyone who wants extra time with me. I also have an "Ask me anything, tell me anything" session on Monday where anyone can come and ask me literally anything. And they do. During the rest of the week, I maintain regular time in the calendar (when it isn't stolen by urgent needs; I'm not perfect) where folks can call me for help. These options allow for my time and energy to be distributed among the team in a more equitable way that triggers less disgust.

Defaulting Is All Around Us

Examples of the Default Effect abound. One is the opt-in/opt-out choice we make with organ donation.[1] Most people support the concept of organ donation in the United States, yet the default choice is to opt *out*, and so most people just go with the default option because it does not require action. In other countries, opting *in* is the default choice, which may explain why some nations have higher rates of organ donation than the US.

A colleague and friend of mine, Liz, recently came up against this default choice with her mum who had been on dialysis for several years and was also diagnosed with early signs of vascular dementia. When she died, the family realized her brain and kidneys could be helpful for scientific research. Unfortunately, there was no way to "untick" the box, and the default option kicked in, preventing her organs from helping save other lives.

Car insurance plans can be a minefield of opt-ins, add-ons, and extra riders where it becomes difficult to understand everything you're signing up for and whether you're getting the best price for what you need. It's often easier to keep things simple and just go with whatever options are pre-selected for you, even if this may not be the best plan for you.

This happens with new vehicles and homes in planned developments as well. People tend to prefer their options grouped into a few pre-chosen "packages" rather than to make all the individual choices themselves. The brain doesn't like to be confused, so the simpler the choices, the happier it is. That way, it can keep the body calm, relaxed, and in homeostasis.

The Default Effect and Our Brain

Some of the first research on the Default Effect Bias was done by W. Samuelson and R. Zeckhauser, who wrote a paper in 1988, "Status Quo Bias in Decision Making." Status quo framing—making one option the default choice—was researched by administering a questionnaire to participants and asking them to make various hypothetical decisions.[2] The finding was that people stick disproportionately to the status quo option.

A separate study was done in which participants were distracted by demanding tasks and given the choice of two snacks. They were more likely to choose the snack they saw a previous participant choose.[3]

The history of the Default Effect Bias goes back, like many of the other biases we've talked about, to early survival mechanisms. Before we had computers and emails, it was easiest to go along with the status quo in order to fit in with the tribe. If you had a different opinion or way of doing things, that could cause conflict and might lead to your being thrown out of the group. Conformity was considered safe, and still is. This explains how truly bizarre ideas can sometimes gain social popularity. It also helps explain the *Keeping Up with the Joneses* phenomenon in which people are motivated to buy the same things they see their neighbors owning.

Any time our brain must go into decision mode, it can get stressed out. The brain likes to keep us from entering a state of anxiety—the so-called fight, flight, or freeze modes. Companies know this. That's why difficult decisions and purchases, such as selecting energy or cable providers or choosing our retirement contribution, are often made *for* us by salesmen eager to close deals. The end result may not be what's best for *us* but what's best for *them*. To know when the Default Effect is at work or being used against us, let's examine a few ideas.

Cognitive effort

When conflicted between two options, it may feel like too much effort to perform explicit evaluations. In such cases, the individual often forgoes explicit evaluations and just picks the default option.[4] It's simply too much work to consider every facet and angle. For example, when choosing between two health insurance plans for employees, we might simply go with the provider that has a familiar name, regardless of whether its plan is superior.

Cost of switching

If by switching away from the default choice, we incur costs, then our brain's rationale is to stick with the default option. Not only might the costs of switching from the default perhaps include paying someone to research alternatives or hiring a consultant, but it's also added stress on our mind. We don't want to invest the time or effort into researching something better when there are other things on our plate that are more immediate. If we decide it will cost too much time, money, or effort to find an alternative—even one that may save us money in the long run—we will likely pick the default. Things like investment plans and other financial vehicles often require a high level of understanding or specialized knowledge and can take large amounts of time and mental capacity away from what we need to do each day.

Loss aversion

Studies show that our thoughts and behaviors are more influenced by avoiding losses than by seeking gains.[5] When evaluating multiple options, the default or current option gains tremendous favor simply by having already been chosen. We'll compare the other options with the default to see what we might lose by making the new choice. We don't feel a need to justify why the default is the best choice—just to analyze why the other options will cause us perceived losses.

When considering using a new supplier or vendor, for instance, there may be potential losses associated with each of the new candidates. The possibility of loss creates anxiety. That's reason enough, in our minds, to stick with the old vendor, even though we might save money and gain efficiencies in the long run with a new one.

Nudge theory

The Default Effect is often taken advantage of in strategic interactions where people are specifically trained to capitalize on it, such as in sales. It's in a company's best interest to ensure that its most profitable options are presented as the default choice. As a simple example, a store may place an item in a convenient place for you to buy it on impulse, even if it isn't the best deal. Discount and outlet stores bet on your tendency to assume that because you are shopping at a "discount store," you are automatically saving money. Often, however, when you find the same item in a regular store, you realize you didn't save as much as you thought. When presenting business deals and organizational changes, parties will strive to frame their preferred outcome as the default choice which incentivizes you to think items will only get more expensive or worse the more you dig instead of better. It is always wise to be wary of falling prey to this bias.

Overcoming This Bias

Lazy-minded leaders fail to check their biases and end up leading passively. They spend little time doing research or making comparisons. They look to what other managers and companies are doing. They go with trends. When it comes to making important decisions, they often make them quickly or allow other people to make them, without putting much thought into whether the decision is the best one for their team or their business. They miss out on Equity by relying on equality—the default choice—which does not serve the team's best interests individually.

CAREing leaders, by contrast, are able to recognize the power of this bias, and they work toward countering it. This entails taking the time to weigh all the options carefully and give them due consideration. Slow is smooth; smooth is fast. Avoid assumptions. Talk to your team about what *they* want. Adapting to their needs will pay dividends.

Choosing the default is usually easier. But when was easy ever best? Opting for an unconventional alternative may require us to go slightly out of our way, even if it's something as simple as asking for proposals from competing vendors. But the benefits can be enormous.

As leaders, it is our job to be conscious choosers. That means researching options (or assigning team members to research them), soliciting feedback from our team, and then making firm decisions. If we don't do this, then companies and salesmen that may not have our best interests at heart will end up making all our decisions for us.

Let's Work It

I'm going to recommend an exercise, knowing you may not do it. Take a careful look at one of your standard default financial decisions: auto insurance.

Write down the last time you looked at your car insurance plan in detail. When was the last time you reviewed your coverages? Consider the many changes that have happened in your life that will cause you to want this to switch. Or reconsider the options if you haven't already done so, especially if it's been more than five years.

Next is to open your account and review your coverage. Review everything that's covered. Do they still make sense based on, say, the age of the vehicle or your financial or family situation? Write down what you like about your policy, what you don't know about it, and what you feel you don't need anymore.

When was the last time you shopped around to see competitors' plans? Often, it's not until we purchase something new that we actually look at options—and even then, we may just go with the company we know because it's easier.

Push your brain to spend some time researching and comparing what competitors offer or even the different policies at your current insurance. What do competitors offer that you like/dislike from your current policy? Is it more in line with your personal needs and financial needs?

What if your age bracket, change in zip code, driving-safety record, change in the number of children driving the car, etc. could make a difference? Even if you don't want to change insurance companies, you can at least call someone in your current company to make sure you are getting the best coverage possible.

This exercise can extend to your homeowners' insurance, investment portfolio, life insurance, disability insurance, or anything else you have been "opting" in or out of by default. Review your bank account and credit cards to see how many recurring charges there are. Have you signed up for any services online that you no longer use (or didn't even know you purchased)? I can practically guarantee that if you do this exercise, you'll put some money back in your pocket—money you can use for things that actually enhance your life.

Finally, share your experience with your team as an example of combatting the Default Effect, and encourage them to do the same. When you get more comfortable with this idea, ask your team to apply it to something in the workplace that has been working okay but could use a potential fix.

START-STOP-CONTINUE EXERCISE

Before we move on to the final bias affecting our ability to provide Equity to our teams, ask yourself these start-stop-continue questions:

Start—*What am I not doing that I need to* start *doing, to challenge the Default Effect Bias in myself and my team?*

Stop—*What am I currently doing that I need to* stop *doing, to challenge the Default Effect Bias in myself and my team?*

Continue—*What am I currently doing that I should* continue *doing, to challenge the Default Effect Bias in myself and my team?*

The final bias is called Extension Neglect. And you'd be amiss to neglect it! You can't miss any part of the CARE Equation if you want to get to the higher performance you want from your team.

CHAPTER 14

EQUITY BIAS #2
EXTENSION NEGLECT

Typical scenario: your boss reads the latest *Harvard Business Review* (HBR) article. Boss takes copious notes on how her team should implement the ideas into its already working systems. In the Monday morning meeting, your boss tells the team they need to read the HBR article and figure out how to apply it to their entire business unit. Everyone sighs. The CAREless boss . . . in action again.

Welcome to the cognitive bias known as "Extension Neglect," which essentially means falling in love with new strategies and solutions without duly considering whether they apply to your situation. This often occurs when you read about a strategy, product, or service that worked for someone else, and you infer that it will work for you, regardless of the fact that the sample size of the original group was quite small or from a different industry or demographic.

Extension Neglect

When Covid tore up our business model of in-person-only leadership training, innovation and quick experimentation was key. I read a lot and was always bringing ideas to the team on how to "do this" or "do that." In rethinking how we market, I came to the team with another idea, only to be told:

"Alex, this isn't going to work. There is no evidence this strategy will be successful." "Evidence?" I said. "There's plenty of evidence! It worked for my friend's company; it'll work for us. A B2C model is where it's at. Trust me!"

Nope. Wrong again. Moving from a business to business (B2B) model to a business to consumer (B2C) model to market our new virtual products turned out to be disastrous. And the misguided effort burned out a team member who felt an immense amount of unfairness in being asked to do something that had little chance of success.

The bias: We assume what works for a sample group will work for everyone else.

The effect on Equity: We make bad decisions for our team based on samples that are unrepresentative or poorly applicable to our situation.

The cure: *Stop* jumping on trends and overextrapolating data. *Start* slowing down, considering your unique situation, and asking your team to keep you honest.

A simple example involves looking at online reviews for restaurants. You find an eatery that looks promising and tell your spouse, "Hey, this place gets five stars; let's try it," without considering that the five-star rating is based on only six reviews and that those six reviewers may have been friends of the chef or drunk college students (not seasoned diners such as yourself). Or remember that Christmas sweater you got from your grandma? Her friends at bingo thought it was adorable. You, on the other hand, wouldn't wear it even if you were paid to!

A more potentially damaging Extension Neglect situation is when a business leader reads a pop-psychology or leadership book or article with a headline announcing, "Millennial Workers Are Looking for [x] from Their Employers," or "The Five Keys to Improving Engagement." The article is loosely inspired by some new business-school study, and the leader takes it at face value. They don't bother to learn that the study cited in the article:

- had more nuanced, less clear-cut results than the headline or article suggests;
- didn't have participants from their industry;
- was conducted in a foreign market; and
- offered barely any significant data.

And a whole other host of factors. But before questioning and considering the article for their team, they try to apply these limited and questionable "findings" to their own team's circumstances, causing grief and confusion and later discovering they don't work at all.

Extension Neglect often impels leaders to implement inequitable solutions. A typical "one-size-does-not-fit-all" example is companies that either push their teams to work remotely or require everyone to come to the office, without regard for individual make-up or the company's specific needs. The pandemic has

> A typical "one-size-does-not-fit-all" example is companies that either push their teams to work remotely or require everyone to come to the office.

brought remote work into the mainstream, but still, you could never hire an auto mechanic to work online. Conversely, forcing people who work best in a quiet, private space—writers or designers, for example—to waste two hours each day commuting to a noisy, distracting office might work for another company, but it might make your people miserable and cause you to lose 30 percent of their productivity.

Extension Neglect Alexample

I can't tell you how many times I have screwed up with this bias. I once purchased a yearly subscription to MasterClass for each of my team members as a Christmas gift, assuming that because two business buddies of mine loved it and got value from it, everyone else would too. They didn't. I wasted money, time, and effort, and my team received a useless gift instead of something they could have actually used.

I also once purchased a self-help daily inspiration calendar for each team member to help them with their life goals. *I* thought it was amazing, so I assumed everyone else would too. Of course, they smiled to my face, but inside they were thinking, *"What am I going to do with this rock-in-a-box?"* Those calendars sit unused on shelves to this day—monuments to Extension Neglect.

When I was forcing my "good ideas" down my teams' throats and assuming that what was good for me—or good for some other company I read about—would be good for them, was I *really* thinking about them or myself? How equitable was that approach?

Our "Storytelling" Brains

We are particularly vulnerable to this bias when information is presented to us in story form. The human brain has a built-in love of storytelling. When we hear stories, parts of our brain "light up." Our hippocampus is activated as well as our frontal and parietal cortices. Stories that contain a good dramatic arc cause our "feel-good" oxytocin levels to rise, along with our empathy response.[1] Stories are far more powerful to our brains than bland information. Stories pull data together in meaningful ways that add up to more than the sum of their parts. When someone tells us a story, our brains mirror the story's cognitive inputs and, to a certain degree, we "experience" the events.

So, it's natural that when we hear an inspiring keynotes speaker at a conference or read/hear a business story that fires us up, we try to relate that story back to our own situation and find applications and connections. Oftentimes, we bend our situation to fit the story rather than bend the story to fit our situation. Remember, the brain is lazy and wants to do things the quickest and easiest way, and changing a whole story certainly isn't easy.

That's why evaluating new information, speculating its applicability, and deconstructing the story in which it was presented to you is important. This can be difficult to do and can also be a hassle, but it's important to be realistic and to pick and choose only those elements of an idea that are applicable to your current and future situation(s). You must force yourself to "fall out of love" with the story and do the hard work of asking yourself questions. And lots of them.

1. **Does this idea really apply to a team like mine?** This is where getting to know your team, your relationships, come into play. You understand the "Who" of the information and the "Who" you are working with. Knowing how your team operates will let you see if this does/doesn't apply to them.

2. **How can I do more research on this idea?** You can go to trusted individuals on your team and see if they know anything about this and how this would land. Setting aside an hour or two to read more about the information would also help and be sure to find different ways this idea has been applied.

3. **Is it logic or emotion that's pushing me to try this?** More self-reflection than anything else, but this helps you consider if you are too involved to see why this can/can't work (think back to the IKEA Effect) or approach it with a good head on your shoulders.

Overcoming this Bias

"I saw a study on how intermittent fasting improves your waistline and gives you more focus. Everyone at the company should try it!"

193

Whenever the "everyone needs to try this" bug strikes you—about any idea or strategy—think about the "E" part of the CARE equation. Equity is about giving people what *they* need, not what you think they need. A strategy may work for some individuals, but to think that everyone should try it neglects to consider the size of the studied team, the industry, or the differences among the types of workers. It also neglects fundamental differences between people. There is no one-size-fits-all pill. Unconscious-bias training for all employees does not make them all less biased.

How do you feel when a friend or spouse "sees the light" and tries to enforce a new lifestyle choice on you? *You need to go carb-free! You need to meditate! You need to try journaling!* Whenever you're trying to force changes on someone else, ask yourself how you felt the last time someone did the same thing to you.

Some things to keep in mind whenever considering a new strategy you want to impose on others:

- Everyone has different backgrounds, personalities, and tastes, as well as different skills and knowledge sets.
- Everyone is at a different stage of their personal/professional development.
- Everyone has different belief systems.
- "One person's meat is another person's poison."
- Everyone is not . . . um, *you.*

A strategy that's effective for one team or brand or company won't necessarily be effective for your team just because you read a sexy article about it. Imposing ideas on team members because they worked somewhere else triggers unfairness in the brain. And unfairness triggers disgust.

One way you can get a handle of this bias is allowing room for people to voice their thoughts before implementing a new strategy. At DX, there's now a "parking lot" in my Teams chat, where I can safely "park" my ideas for people to read and react to before we implement them. We only try the ones that survive scrutiny. Consider creating your own "parking lot" where ideas get "polished" before you try them. Maybe it's that business book you think everyone should read or the list of "cool" new ideas your HR team just brought back from a conference they attended. New ideas should definitely be tried, but let people weigh in on them first and offer their perspectives.

Get together with your team and gather their feedback or send out a memo outlining the idea you're considering implementing and ask for everyone's response. This will create more trust and credibility for you, as you won't always be jumping into new strategies that don't work.

The next time you come across a study, program, or system you're sure will be a great fit for the team, slow down and think about it. That includes books . . . even this one! I've spent fourteen chapters telling you about mistakes I've made, lessons I've learned, and biases I've been working on. I've shown you how I applied my CAREful thinking within my team at DX Learning with successful results. But that doesn't mean any of my examples or pieces of specific advice apply to your company or your life. Only you, as their leader, can determine that.

Let's Work It

As James Clear explains in his book *Atomic Habits*, the aim is to get at least 1 percent better every day. You do that and you will be thirty-seven times improved by the end of the year. I've taken this idea to heart, so every time I read *Harvard Business Review, Inc.* magazine, or a new book, I list out all the potential actions I can apply to improve me or the business.

Now, I want you to consider what you have learned from reading this book so far. We've talked about how to provide more Clarity to your team, give Autonomy, establish Relationships, and supply Equity to everyone based on their needs. Have you created a list of to-do's for any of these ideas? A list of actions that you want to implement? I truly hope you have at least one action that you want to work on from reading this book. Take a minute and write down one goal for each part of the CARE Equation we've talked about. From that, pick one of those ideas and make it your goal to get 1 percent better . . .

After you pick that idea, ask yourself these questions to keep you from falling into your biases:

If I were to go and apply it to my team right now, how would it be received?

What assumptions am I making?

Am I falling into any of the potential biases?

How do I know it will work?

Who can I ask to make sure before I apply this idea that I know it will land as I want it to?

START-STOP-CONTINUE EXERCISE

As we wrap up this final chapter on the CARE Equation, here's one last round of questions for you to answer to drive this last point home.

Start—*What am I not doing that I need to* start *doing, to reduce Extension Neglect in myself and my team?*

Stop—*What am I currently doing that I need to* stop *doing, to reduce Extension Neglect in myself and my team?*

Continue—*What am I currently doing that I should* continue *doing, to reduce Extension Neglect in myself and my team?*

ON EQUITY

Equity is about providing the people you serve with a sense of fairness so that your team can be at cognitive ease. Equity is really the gauge of higher performance. Equitable leadership is treating people how *they* want to be treated, not how *you* want to be treated. This personalized approach to leadership ensures balance for your team. It's not easy, but the easiest way is rarely the best way.

Remember:

CLARITY is the WHAT.

AUTONOMY is the HOW.

RELATIONSHIPS are the WHO.

EQUITY is the WANT.

Intentional and customized resource allocation leads to psychological safety. That means you should think about the humans you're serving before taking action. If you don't—if you get this wrong in a big or continual way—your people will be on LinkedIn looking for new jobs. If you get this right consistently, you will create a team culture where everyone has one another's back. You'll create a "we versus me" mentality. By treating people how they want to be treated, you allow them to be their authentic selves and capitalize on what makes them unique and set them up to win. That's the secret sauce of psychological safety and the fuel for high performance. Do it right, and people openly help each other out. They will give spare time and resources to other team members that need it. Do it wrong, and it's each person for themselves. That

doesn't help you create a higher-performing team that will break down walls for each other. You can't be high-performing all by yourself, or with only one or two rock stars. So much more gets done with a *team* of rock stars.

CHAPTER 15

PUTTING IT ALL
TOGETHER

CARE is simple. Simple to remember. Simple to understand. Simple to think about. Simple to apply and explain to others. It is an equation where if a letter is missing or doesn't add up and there is imbalance, then you don't get the end result you expected.

The CARE Equation:

- By slowing down and giving yourself and your team the right levels of Clarity (C), you establish crystal clear goals and parameters. *"What"* your employees need to do and *"What"* you need is clear to them. Done right, and they will ask questions to clear up any grey area until you are both aligned.
- With everyone on the same line of the same page of the same book, you can grant people the Autonomy (A) they need to work in their own entrusted way based on their preferences. *"How"* they get work done is up to them, and you serve as a resource during

this process so they feel in control while knowing they can rely on you. "A" leads to you doing less of the work yourself where you head is down "in" the weeds, which opens up more time for you to be above the work and do what is really important.

- You now have the time and presence to build stronger Relationships (R) with those you serve and to discover who they are and what motivates them. WHO you are working with is just as important as WHAT you are working on. Relationships build trust and are the key to psychological safety and higher performance.
- Armed with the knowledge of what motivates and drives your team members at work and at home, you can now provide tailored Equity (E), distributing your time, energy, and resources to those who need what at the right levels. That means treating people the way they WANT to be treated and providing them with what they need to succeed, not the way you want to be treated or what you think they need. The more Equity you have in a team, the more it multiplies C, A and R. It's the real gauge for higher performance. And the more you become the selfless, CAREing leader people will remember you as, the closer you are to winning.

C + A + R + E = CARE

In reality, of course, the steps don't always unfold in such neat chronological order. C→A→R→E is how the steps work together, conceptually, to support one another. Sometimes you may need to work on the R before you can tailor an approach to C and A and find a better balance in E. And even the formula itself is not a one-size-fits-all approach.

While every human in the world craves Clarity, Autonomy, and Relationships, not everyone craves them in the same amounts and proportions. I am an entrepreneur who is comfortable dealing with chaos on the fly, and so I don't require as much Clarity as my aforementioned COO who gets very upset when I don't meet their clearness expectations. That doesn't make me right and them wrong or vice versa. My job is simply to give them what they want, not want I want. I have a high craving for Autonomy. But not everyone is like me. If I give too much Autonomy to someone who wants more guidance, they will become stressed and miserable.

The real magic in the CARE Equation is to know your team members' preferences for Clarity, Autonomy, and Relationships. There is no one-size-fits-all. It's discovering and consistently adapting to the preferences of those you serve—not assuming what people need for them. That's where you get the Equity from. It's the gauge that shows you how effectively you are using Clarity, Autonomy, and Relationships to bring your team psychological safety and lead them to higher performance. That means working through your biases to reduce your assumptions as well as any perceived threats to those you serve. This requires time and intentionality. If you do this effectively and consistently, Equity is felt, your team members are at cognitive ease, and you have embraced the four essentials of psychological safety, thereby inspiring a high-performing team.

Psychological safety is what we're aiming for. Why? Let's go back to the definition used by Amy Edmondson, the top researcher on the subject. Psychological safety is "a shared belief held by members of a team that the team is safe for interpersonal risk-taking." Risk is the critical element here. Only when a team feels safe to take risks will they come forward with their best ideas, will they bring their full selves and their whole range of talents to work, will they ask critical questions, and will they be willing to fail fast and fail often to get to the best solutions. Psychological safety takes the blinders off and allows teams to rise to their highest possible performance levels.

CARE is what leads to psychological safety. Clarity provides people safety and well-defined parameters in which to operate, letting them take contained risks. Autonomy gives them the freedom to experiment and tells them they are trusted by leadership. Having well-built Relationships assures everyone their authentic selves are treasured. And Equity says they'll be given the support and resources they need when *they* need them.

Psychological safety and high performance are joined at the hip. When your team is in a place of psychological safety, they will then tell you when you get it wrong. They will tell you what is missing. They will tell you what to do more of and less of. They will tell you when there is a problem. They will offer new ideas. They will challenge stale thinking. They will ask for more responsibility, knowing they won't get their heads chopped off if they make a mistake. They will not fall into the trap of deadly silence that kills leadership, that kills relationships, that kills business.

High-performing teams need high-performing leaders.

High-performing leaders need high-performing teams.

Higher performance comes from everyone CAREing to win.

Your role in this?

YOU Complete the Equation

Think of yourself as a master Uber driver. Your job is to drive the car the way your passengers want it driven, not the way you like to drive. If you routinely drive fast, but the passenger does not like to go fast, they will be holding on to their seat belt with white knuckles, too scared to say anything. But if you ask them first and *learn* how they like to be driven, and then honor their preferences, they will feel secure and will be much more likely to open up. The two of you can then become better aligned on the destination. By listening to them, you might discover a route that's more efficient. You might even learn something about the passenger which allows you to better connect with them. The result is they won't run for the hills when they get out of the car. They may even request you as their Uber driver next time.

As you are striving to become a great, psychologically safe leader (i.e., Uber driver) for those around you, don't forget: you are a passenger in the car as well. You are an integral part of the team. You cannot expect of others what you will not do yourself. And you cannot give to others without letting others give to you.

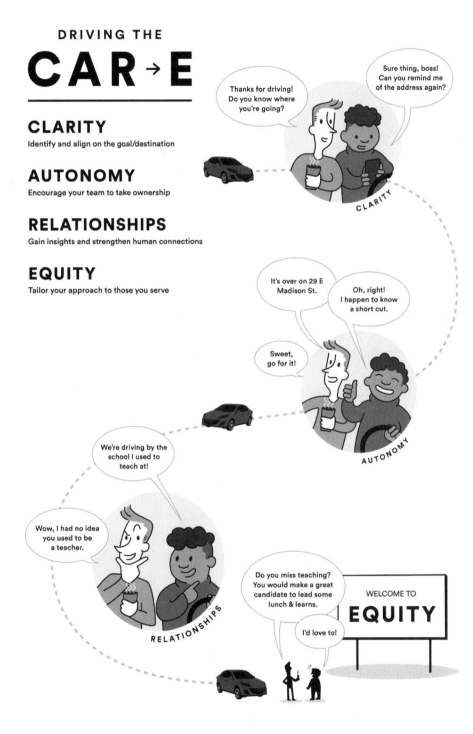

DX lost money in 2018, 2019, 2020 and 2021. I'd started the company with my own money and had taken out significant loans to keep the lights on. My son was born in 2017 and my daughter in 2018, just as the headaches of growing an organization began kicking in. The pandemic ripped my business to shreds, and we had to start over again. And I was dealing with many other issues, including the writing of this book and family challenges back in the UK. Suffice it to say, life was stressful, and I had a lot to worry about. So much so that in May of 2022, while driving from the suburbs of Chicago to work in downtown, my brain and body shut down in the middle of a busy highway.

When I regained consciousness after a few seconds, I pulled over to gather myself, then carefully drove home where I lay on my bed thinking every negative thought imaginable. Years of stress had finally caught up with me. I was on the verge of a mental breakdown, and my mind and body were saying *enough is enough*. I knew it was time to slow down, stop trying to play Superman, and just be human—vulnerable, imperfect, and limited. I needed to tell my team what I was going through.

The following Monday, our morning team call was about to start, and I knew this would be a good time to let them know what I was going through. I planned what I was going to say, and then . . . nothing! I couldn't do it. *"What will they think?"* my mind whispered to me. *"They can't see me this way." "If I show weakness, I won't be a leader. They need me to be strong."*

I remained silent—which went against the whole premise of psychological safety and the culture we were trying to build.

Tuesday rolled around. Another chance to let the team know. Again, my brain got the better of me. Silence. Same thing on Wednesday.

Three days of silence. Three days of the team thinking everything was dandy in my life. Three days of coming apart at the seams, needing help, and failing to ask for it. Finally, on Thursday, I sent an email. It was easier to put my thoughts in writing than to express them verbally. Here is that email (unedited, in its raw and messy form):

Subject: Better to know than not

Team, I am not good with this stuff, but feel its best you know than not. Last Monday while I was driving to work I just broke down. I had to stop the car and drive home. Curled up in bed until the 10am call. I think it was just a mental breakdown from all the stuff I am dealing with. I will deal with it and on the outside all will be good, but on the inside there is pain and I am not at my best. There is no ask, just knowledge. My leadership has not, and will not be where it needs to be and I am sorry for not being at my best and there for you, which is one of the factors.

Other factors are a combo of the fact I am working more hours than I have ever worked, with more stress and worry than even during the dark days of the pandemic. A friend I knew took his life last week. Putin, the risk of nuclear war and what's happening in Ukraine. The financial meltdown that is getting worse. Breakdown of key family relationships. The son of my late sister who took her life, calling my Dad 2 weeks ago and his reaction, unlocking old family wounds. Having to re-write the whole book and finding the time to do that. Not being present when I need to be for my kids due to worry about the business and its finances and not being the Dad I want to be, and the to-do lists that only get longer. The new family set up with my wife's job. And many other things I am dealing with seem to have caught up to me.

I wanted to say this while talking on Monday and Wednesday, but the words wouldn't come out. So reverting to doing it this way. I wanted you to know in case it happens again, or I am short with you, say something I shouldn't etc. I am probably having a bad day. I will be back and please be patient. I promise to get back to the good times and be the leader that models our values. Thanks for your patience.

Kill it today.

Alex

The replies from the team were unforgettable. So kind, so compassionate, so full of understanding and CARE. Here is one team member's reply (also presented unedited):

Echoing the thoughts of those before - you are just human.

Although . . . sometimes I think you are NOT if I am being perfectly honest . . . like how the F*@k does this guy get all this shit done? What drugs is he taking? Where can I get them?

Even if you are part alien, the human side is what binds us all. Burnout is all too real. We got your back. You've started and continue to effectively lead a badass company where the sky is the limit. We all take pride in DX and what we do for the world and that's thanks to you.

Empathy is the metaskill of the ~~20th~~ 21st no . . . hell . . . it's just THE human metaskill. Quickest way for empathy to happen is through vulnerability, so thank you for sharing. We will be better because of it. I hope you know whatever you need from us, I am confident you can pick up the phone to any of your employees and ask for anything . . . or just have ANY conversation. How many bosses can say that? That›s because of the team and company you›ve created and helped us build alongside you.

What's the lesson here? People can't help *us* if they don't know we need help. If I had remained silent about what I was facing, no one would have known, and nothing would have changed. But something *did* change that day.

> People can't help *us* if they don't know we need help.

CAREing came full circle and rescued me from the brink. A problem shared is a problem more likely to be solved. That's the power of speaking up early and speaking up often.

Silence kills organizations. Silence kills leadership. Silence kills relationships. Silence kills.

We need to remove fearful silence from the workplace and from life. That includes *you*, as the leader. You are the final piece of the CARE Equation. When you CARE for your team fully, they will CARE for you in return. And you absolutely must let them. When you become a recipient of this type of CAREing, you remove the final bit of blockage and resistance from the system. You allow your team to give back to you which completes the cycle and opens up a circular flow. You satisfy their need to be CARE*ers* as well as CARE*ees* and unleash some of their leadership potential in the process.

And that, my friend, is the essence of high performance: everyone leading from where they sit or stand and CAREing for one another in a virtuous cycle—an upwardly spinning spiral that lifts everyone in its path and inspires everyone to be their very best.

The Power of Vulnerability

You've no doubt noticed in this book that I tell a lot of stories about my own struggles. There is purpose behind that. That is my style of leadership. I am open about my mistakes because I expect others to be. My hope is that the vulnerability and humility I exhibit will create the environment for others to lean into their own vulnerability and humility. A culture of openness is what I am going for. Openness, in my opinion, is everything.

(C + A + R + E) * V = CARE in its highest form (V= vulnerability)

The culture of a team is a mirror of its leadership. Leadership is how you think and behave. What you value drives how you think and behave. If you value silence and complacency and are comfortable with a rotating staff, that's what you'll lead like, and that's what your team or organization will be like. If you value openness, honesty, and progress, that's what you'll lead like. That's what your team or organization will be like.

For others to speak up, you need to set the example of speaking up (for) yourself. You cannot expect of others what you are not willing to do yourself. If you want your team to feel safe taking risks, you must take personal risks too. If you want your team to be honest, you must model honesty. If you want your team to be open and vulnerable, you must be open and vulnerable.

Vulnerability is a non-negotiable in the quest for psychological safety and higher performance. It is table stakes. Without vulnerability, you can try to CARE all you want, but it won't earn you any more than what you started with. When vulnerability is not modeled and expected, people stay silent. Out of fear. And as I think I may have mentioned before, but just to give you some more Clarity . . . silence kills.

When vulnerability is championed, embraced, and lived, the conditions are ripe for CARE to blossom. Openness reigns. You can now build a psychologically safe vessel in which to fly your team to new heights of performance and CARE to Win every single day. The sky is the limit.

END

APPENDIX:
CARE QUESTIONS

Questions can make or break a leader. It can make or break a team. Remember: silence kills organizations. Silence kills leadership. Silence kills relationships. To gauge how well you are CAREing for those you serve, answer yes/no to the ideas below. There is no gray area here. You are either effective, or you are not. It's ok not to be effective right now; what's more important is that you start to think about what you can do to get better. These are the leading indicators of CARE that you can control. What are your strengths and weaknesses?

Clarity
- I always effectively communicate the team's goals and objectives.
- The goals I set are always measurable and attainable.
- I am highly skilled at explaining the purpose and significance of the team's goals.
- I encourage open communication about my team's goals and invite feedback.
- I ensure that everyone on the team knows what is expected of them in achieving their goals.
- I am receptive to questions and clarifications related to my team's goals.

- I always keep my team informed about what is going on in our organization.
- I always make an effort to explain how a task or project relates to the bigger picture when discussing tasks or projects.

Autonomy

- I provide opportunities for professional growth and encourage my team to take on new challenges.
- I consistently trust my team to handle tasks without micromanaging every step of the process.
- I provide resources and guidance but allow my team to determine the best course of action.
- My team has a sense of ownership and accountability for the outcomes of their work.
- I value and listen to my team's input when making important decisions.
- My team has the necessary authority they need to do their jobs well.
- I go out of my way to understand each team member's point of view.
- My team can take risks at work that could lead to important new products, services, or solutions.
- I encourage new ideas on my team that defy conventional wisdom.

Relationships

- I always foster a positive and inclusive team culture.
- My team feels a very strong sense of belonging and camaraderie.
- My team feels comfortable discussing both personal and work-related matters with me.
- I actively promote teamwork and encourage collaboration among team members.
- My team always feels comfortable providing constructive feedback to anyone on our team.

- I care greatly about my team's overall well-being.
- My team is extremely satisfied with the cooperation they receive from colleagues.
- On my team, people are always treated with respect.
- All my team members have a friend at work who they share new ideas with.

Equity

- I always treat people fairly at work.
- My team can trust me to be fair to everyone on our team.
- My team all feel like they are valued.
- I provide each member of my team with opportunities to balance their work life and personal life.
- I delegate tasks based on each individual's strengths and expertise.
- I ensure that resources and opportunities are distributed fairly among team members.
- I consider the workload and individual circumstances of each associate when assigning resources.
- I am always approachable and responsive when team members need assistance.
- My team is always committed to doing quality work.

Psychological Safety[1]

- If you make a mistake on this team, it is often held against you.
- Members of this team are able to bring up problems and tough issues.
- People on this team sometimes reject others for being different.
- It is safe to take a risk on this team.
- It is difficult for team members to get help from one another.
- No one on this team would deliberately act in a way that undermines each other's efforts.
- Working with members of this team, I make sure their unique skills and talents are valued and utilized.

The questions below will get you to think about the lagging indicators of CARE. How witnessable are these statements in your team? Where are there the strengths and weaknesses? What should you START or STOP doing to level up?

Clarity
- Are people on my team comfortable asking questions if they are unclear on tasks without feeling like they sound out of the loop?
- On my team, do I make an effort to explain the why behind my decisions?
- Does my team understand the goals of the company and where we fit into the bigger picture?
- On my team, are there frequent check-ins to ensure our work product is on target to achieve our collective goals?
- Am I making sure that people on my team are clear on goals, roles, and responsibilities?

Autonomy
- Are the people on my team empowered to approach their work on their own terms?
- Is there a high amount of trust on this team?
- In my team meetings, do I feel as though everyone's opinions have a chance to be voiced and considered?
- Am I encouraging people on my team to explore additional responsibilities or new opportunities?
- Does my team continually make an effort to challenge the status quo?

Relationships
- Do the people on my team collaborate effectively?
- On my team, do people know each other on a personal level, not just professionally?

- Are the people on my team comfortable giving candid feedback, no matter the recipient?
- Is my perspective heard and valued on my team? Do I feel that it is heard and valued?
- Do people on my team make an effort to provide and receive both positive and constructive feedback?

Equity

- Are those on my team receiving resources proportionately to their individual needs?
- Can I expect everyone to say they feel comfortable asking for help?
- Do I feel as though everyone on my team is treated fairly?
- Am I purposefully delegating the work on my team to each employee's strengths, interests, development, and availability in mind?

Psychological Safety

- Does my team shows empathy for each other consistently and authentically?
- Can people on my team comfortably admit their mistakes?
- On my team, am I bringing my authentic self to work?
- Do my team members frequently invite others to challenge their perspectives?
- Am I making people feel comfortable enough to have difficult discussions without fear of negative consequences?
- Does everyone on the team know that if they make a mistake, it won't be held against them? Do I believe this idea, and show it in my actions?

ACKNOWLEDGMENTS

This is my first book. Many times, throughout the process, I vowed this would be my only book! However, seeing it all come together, I don't believe this to be true anymore. Although getting here was way harder than I ever imagined, I now know that nothing good comes easy and that the work was well worth it. So, thank you, coffee, for making this book possible. The idea for this book was hatched before the pandemic, and I started work soon after the lockdown occurred. And here we are, four years later. The list of those who have supported me in this journey is vast.

Firstly, recognition must go out to my first employers, Nigel Downing and Brian Helweg-Larsen. Without them having given me a chance and allowing me the opportunity to move to America in 2005, this book would never have happened. For that, I will be forever thankful.

I would also like to express my sincere gratitude to Andrew Wolfendon. Andrew took a raw and emotional manuscript from someone who had no idea what the hell was going on and used his expertise to help hone it into much of what you see today. He is a true expert at his trade. Big thanks to Liz Wright for working with me to create that raw and emotional manuscript, that without the support of Jesse Krieger would not have happened in the first place.

Science is important to me and my business, DX. As I am not a trained scientist, Ryan Aguiar was my science mentor, researcher, and book-writing sidekick. This book would not have been possible without him. The research into the biases is all his doing. I hope the lessons learned in helping me create this book lead to you writing your own one day. I loved the two-way feedback loop we had in the early days of creating the framework for how the book would pan out. Still intact, my friend. I appreciate you and could not have done this without you.

You cannot build a business without a team. To every DX employee—past, present and future—thank you for learning with me. You have helped me get better every day by giving me feedback on what works and what does not when it comes to CAREing leadership.

I am grateful to all those at Brown Books, especially Sterling Hooker, for giving me a second chance and holding my hand through the tough process of getting this book to the finish line. Sterling and I really worked intensively in the copy edit stage to bring you what you have now. Her enthusiasm for the work truly opened up several new channels of creativity.

I am also thankful to the Bates Meron team for creating the illustrations used throughout the book. Cameryn Berridge, you took those biases and made the content pop visually, bringing the book to life.

I will always be grateful to my family who brought me into the world. My Mum and brothers, Peter and Simon, instilled values that contributed to the human I am today. To my sisters, Rachel and Joss. We have learned the hard way what a lack of vulnerability can do to a human. The heart of this book is harnessing the power of speaking up to be your best self and performing at your best. We have shown what happens when you get over your fears and speak up about what matters. I am a better human because of the two of you. You have always been there for me through thick and thin. Our relationship is the reason I am the leader, husband, and father I am today. You have shown more CARE than you will ever know.

Finally, a heartfelt thank you to Karoline, my wife, for giving me the time and support to write this book. Four years in the making, with two young children, a global pandemic, a business meltdown, publisher bankruptcy, and much more. You kept me going even when I wanted to quit. You made coffee to keep me awake and hugged me when I needed to calm down. You looked after the kids when I needed to get my head down on the weekends and evenings. You sacrificed your time and energy to give me the bandwidth to bring CARE to the world. I will always love you and will always be grateful for your sacrifice. We are polar opposites on each of the CARE spectrums. I have a low craving for clarity; you have high. I want to give Autonomy and control to others freely; you prefer to be in control. I am sometimes frosty on the edges and hard to break down; you want to spill the beans on everything. Yet we are testament to what happens when you have equity in a family. We balance each other out with intentionality and the understanding of our preferences and work hard to speak up early and often to preserve the love we have for one another. I could not have done this without you—my rock.

NOTES

Chapter 1:

1. Emily Kwong, "Understanding Unconscious Bias: Short Wave." *NPR*. Podcast Audio. July 15, 2020. https://www.npr.org/2020/07/14/891140598/understanding-unconscious-bias; Jaimar Tuarez, "How Many Calculations Per Second Can The Human Brain Do?" *NeuroTray*. Updated October 19, 2022. https://neurotray.com/how-many-calculations-per-second-can-the-human-brain-do/
2. Maya Angelou, "They May Forget What You Said, But They Will Never Forget How You Made Them Feel." *Quote Investigator*, April 6, 2014. https://quoteinvestigator.com/2014/04/06/they-feel/

Chapter 2:

1. C. S. Dweck, *Mindset: The New Psychology of Success*. (Oregon: Robinson, 2017).
2. C. Dweck, "What Having a "Growth Mindset" Actually Means." *Harvard Business Review*. January 13, 2016. https://hbr.org/2016/01/what-having-a-growth-mindset-actually-means
3. C. Dweck, "The power of believing that you can improve." TED.com. November 2014. Retrieved December 2, 2021. https://www.ted.com/talks/carol_dweck_the_power_of_believing_that_you_can_improve

4. Dweck, *Mindset*. (Robinson, 2017).
5. Kate Fehlhaber, "Why a bank robber thought covering himself in lemon juice would help him get away with it." *Quartz*. May 19, 2017. https://qz.com/986221/what-know-it-alls-dont-know-or-the-illusion-of-competence
6. J. Kruger and D. Dunning, "Unskilled and unaware of it: How difficulties in recognizing one's own incompetence lead to inflated self-assessments." *Journal of Personality and Social Psychology*. 1999. doi:10.1037/0022-3514.77.6.1121. https://doi.org/10.1037//0022-3514.77.6.1121
7. M. Gladwell, *Outliers: The Story of Success*. (Boston: Back Bay Books, Little, Brown and Company, 2019).

Chapter 3:
1. Melody Wilding, L. M. S. W. "How to be a confident, concise communicator (even when you have to speak off the cuff)." *Forbes*. October 5, 2020. Retrieved December 3, 2021
2. Kim Harrison, "Good internal communication leads to stronger employee engagement and therefore better organizational performance." *Cutting Edge PR*. June 1, 2020. https://cuttingedgepr.com/articles/good-internal-communication-leads-to-stronger-employee-engagement-and-therefore-better-organizational-performance/
3. S. Sinek, *Start with Why: How Great Leaders Inspire Everyone to Take Action*. (London: Portfolio Penguin, 2019.)
4. Sinek, *Start with Why*. (Portfolio Penguin, 2019)

Chapter 4:
1. Elizabeth Louise Newton, "The Rocky Road from Actions to Intentions." PhD dissertation, Standford University. 1990. https://gwern.net/doc/psychology/cognitive-bias/illusion-of-depth/1990-newton.pdf

Chapter 5:
1. Sheena Iyengar and Mark Lepper, "When Choice is Demotivating: Can One Desire Too Much of a Good Thing?" *Journal of Personality and Social Psychology*. 2000. https://faculty.washington.edu/jdb/345/345%20Articles/Iyengar%20%26%20Lepper%20(2000).pdf

2. Shanto Iyengar and Donald Kinder, "The Effects of Framing on Citizen Knowledge of and Support for Social Policies." *American Political Science Review.* 1987.

3. L.G. Block and P.A. Keller, "When to Accentuate the Negative: The Effects of Perceived Efficacy and Message Framing on Intentions to Perform a Health-Related Behavior." *Journal of Marketing Research,* 32(2), 192. 1995. https://doi.org/10.2307/3152047

4. Amos Tversky and D. Kahneman, "The Framing of Decisions and the Psychology of Choice." *Science.* January 30, 1981. doi: 10.1126/science.7455683. PMID: 7455683. https://psych.hanover.edu/classes/Cognition/Papers/tversky81.pdf

Chapter 6:

1. Rick Nauert. n.d. https://psychcentral.com/news/2011/01/25/worker-autonomy-can-lead-to-greater-productivity-satisfaction/22885.html

2. N.a. "Work Design Principle #1: Give Employees More Control over Their Work." Harvard T.H. Chan: The Work and Well-Being Initiative. (n.d.) https://workwellbeinginitiative.org/module-2-enhancing-employee-control-work

3. Michael B. Stanier, *The Advice Trap.* (München: Verlag Franz Vahlen GmbH, 2021).

4. Amy C. Edmondson, *The Fearless Organization: Creating Psychological Safety in the Workplace for Learning, Innovation, and Growth.* (New York: John Wiley & Sons, Inc., 2019)

5. Brené Brown, *Rising Strong* (New York: Random House Publishing Group, 2017).

Chapter 7:

1. Michael Norton, Daneil Mochon, and Dan Ariely, "The IKEA effect: When labor leads to love." *Journal of Consumer Psychology,* 22(3), 453-460. 2012. https://www.hbs.edu/ris/Publication%20Files/11-091.pdf

2. Norton, et al., "The IKEA effect: When labor leads to love." *Journal of Consumer Psychology.* 2012. https://www.sciencedirect.com/science/article/abs/pii/S1057740811000829

3. Daniel Friedman, et al. "Searching for the sunk cost fallacy." *Experimental Economics*, 10(1), 79-104. 2007. https://link.springer.com/article/10.1007/s10683-006-9134-0

Chapter 8:

1. Francesco Marcatto and Donatella Ferrante, "The Regret and Disappointment Scale: An instrument for assessing regret and disappointment in decision making." Cambridge University Press, 3(1), 87. January 1, 2023. https://www.cambridge.org/core/journals/judgment-and-decision-making/article/regret-and-disappointment-scale-an-instrument-for-assessing-regret-and-disappointment-in-decision-making/93535662142D9C8A5DC-B87288E38C23B

2. Rebecca Ratner and Kenneth Herbst. "When good decisions have bad outcomes: The impact of affect on switching behavior." *ScienceDirect*. Organizational Behavior and Human Decision Processes, 96(1), 23-37. 2005. https://www.sciencedirect.com/science/article/abs/pii/S0749597804000767

Chapter 9:

1. T. Allas and B. Schaninger. "Five fifty: Better bosses." McKinsey & Company, September 2020. https://www.mckinsey.com/capabilities/people-and-organizational-performance/our-insights/five-fifty-better-bosses

Chapter 11:

1. R. Matthew Montoya, Robert S. Horton, and Jeffrey Kirchner. "Is actual similarity necessary for attraction? A meta-analysis of actual and perceived similarity." *Sage Journals*, December 1, 2008. https://journals.sagepub.com/doi/10.1177/0265407508096700

2. Jerald Greenberg, *Behavior in organizations: Student value edition.* Perception and Learning: Understanding and Adapting to the Work Environment. Place of publication not identified: Prentice Hall. 2010.

Chapter 12:

1. Corradi-Dell'Acqua, et al., "Cross-modal representations of first-hand and vicarious pain, disgust and fairness in insular and cingulate cortext." *Nature Communications*, 2013; Zhong et al., 2016

2. Mariagiovanna Cantone, et al. "Fear and disgust: case report of two uncommon emotional disturbances evoked by visual disperceptions after a right temporal-insular stroke." *BMC Neurology*, 2019. https://bmcneurol.biomedcentral.com/articles/10.1186/s12883-019-1417-0

3. Ho Namkung, Sun-Hong Kim, and Akira Sawa. "The insula: an underestimated brain area in clinical neuroscience, psychiatry, and neurology." *National Library of Medicine*, 2017. https://www.ncbi.nlm.nih.gov/pmc/articles/PMC5538352

4. Kevin Grossman, "The Fairness Perception Problem Plaguing Recruiting." *ERE*, April 21, 2022. https://www.ere.net/the-fairness-perception-problem-plaguing-recruiting/

5. Brian Kropp, Jessica Knight, and Jonah Shepp. "How Fair Is Your Workplace?" *Harvard Business Review*, July 14, 2022. https://hbr.org/2022/07/how-fair-is-your-workplace

6. Kropp, et al. "How Fair Is Your Workplace?" *Harvard Business Review*, 2022.

Chapter 13:

1. Eric J. Johnson and Daniel G. Goldstein, "Do Defaults Save Lives?" *Science*. 302 (5649): 1338–1339. doi:10.1126/science.1091721. 2009. https://papers.ssrn.com/sol3/papers.cfm?abstract_id=1324774

2. William Samuelson and Richard Zeckhauser, "Status Quo Bias in Decision Making." *Journal of Risk and Uncertainty*, 1(1), 7-59. https://scholar.harvard.edu/rzeckhauser/publications/status-quo-bias-decision-making

3. N.a. "Default Effect." *Psynso*, 2018. https://psynso.com/default-effect/

4. Gerd Gigerenzer, "Why Heuristics Work." Perspectives on Psychological Science. *Sage Journals*. 3 (1): 20–281. doi:10.1111/j.1745-6916.2008.00058.x. 2008. https://journals.sagepub.com/doi/abs/10.1111/j.1745-6916.2008.00058.x

5. Amos Tversky and Daniel Kahneman. "Loss Aversion in Riskless Choice: A Reference-Dependent Model." *The Quarterly Journal of Economics.* 106 (4): 1039. 1991. https://www.sscnet.ucla.edu/polisci/faculty/chwe/austen/tversky1991.pdf

Chapter 14:

1. Paul J. Zak, "Why Inspiring Stories Make Us React: The Neuroscience of Narrative." *PubMed Central,* 2015. https://www.ncbi.nlm.nih.gov/pmc/articles/PMC4445577

Appendix:

1. Amy C. Edmondson, *The Fearless Organization: Creating Psychological Safety in the Workplace for Learning, Innovation, and Growth.* (New York: John Wiley & Sons, Inc., 2019)

ABOUT THE AUTHOR

Alex started life as a trainee schoolteacher in the UK. In 2002 he moved into adult education when he joined a global management training organization. In 2005 he moved to Chicago to build and lead the company's operation in America. It was there he found his passion and purpose around developing people's leadership capabilities (EQ) versus management skills (IQ), and in 2015 he started his own organization, DX, built on these ideas. DX combines human capital optimization with progressive leadership development to expose and eliminate toxicity and prepare organizations, leaders, and teams to put people first and create companies worth working for. In using his CARE Equation, Alex has helped develop and unlock leadership potential in over forty thousand people through DX's keynotes, conferences, offsites, retreats, and leadership development programs all over the world, building a human-centric movement while still being a people-first leader himself both at work and at home.